STOCK MARKET INVESTING FOR BEGINNERS

UNBREAKABLE RULES YOU NEED FOR STOCK TRADING AND INVESTING

Perfect For Swing and Day Trading Options, Futures, Forex and Cryptocurrencies

Wild Horse Media Publications

WILLIAM   KERKOVAN

© Copyright 2019 by William Kerkovan - All rights reserved.

This document is geared towards providing exact and reliable information in regards to the topic and issue covered. The publication is sold with the idea that the publisher is not required to render accounting, officially permitted, or otherwise, qualified services. If advice is necessary, legal or professional, a practiced individual in the profession should be ordered.

From a Declaration of Principles which was accepted and approved by a Committee of the American Bar Association and a Committee of Publishers and Associations.

In no way is it legal to reproduce, duplicate, or transmit any part of this document in either electronic means or in printed format. Recording of this publication is strictly prohibited and any storage of this document is not allowed unless with written permission from the publisher. All rights reserved.

The information provided herein is stated to be truthful and consistent, in that any liability, in terms of inattention or otherwise, by any usage or abuse of any policies, processes, or directions contained within is the solitary and utter responsibility of the recipient reader. Under no circumstances will any legal responsibility or blame be held against the publisher for any reparation, damages, or monetary loss due to the information herein, either directly or indirectly.

Respective authors own all copyrights not held by the publisher.

The information herein is offered for informational purposes solely, and is universal as so. The presentation of the information is without contract or any type of guarantee assurance.

The trademarks that are used are without any consent, and the publication of the trademark is without permission or backing by the trademark owner. All trademarks and brands within this book are for clarifying purposes only and are owned by the owners themselves, not affiliated with this document.

This Page Has Been Intentional Left Blank

By The Way

Please Visit The Audible Store For An AudioBook Version Of This Book

Table of Contents

Introduction 1

Chapter 1: Rule Number One (Don't Leave Home Without Doing It) 7

Chapter 2: Rule Number Two (Do This And Better Your Chances To Win) 30

Chapter 3: Rule Number Three (Things Which You Want To Know) 51

Chapter 4: Rule Number Four (Facts And Numbers To Help You) 95

Chapter 5: Rule Number Five (Master The Mystic Arts) 120

Chapter 6: Rule Number Six (Constant Profits) 155

Conclusion 167

Introduction

Hello. It seems that you are likely to be having the same thoughts or intentions as myself when I first got bitten by the investing and trading bug. I would venture so far as to say this because how else would you be reading this at this very moment if it weren't for the desire for knowledge about the stock market and other financial instruments. Even more so, I would say, would be the want and hunger for specific knowledge on how to make money and create wealth from the same said markets. Am I not right?

I had those exact same thoughts when I was but in high school. It started out as something fluid and intangible, where I just had this tingling bit of excitement at the thought of making some dough just by choosing the right shares and clicking the right buttons. Yes. I am not of the generation where exchanges were dominated by men shouting and yelling. By the time I made my first foray into the stock market, the digital age had already dawned on the financial markets. I am not that old, but daresay old enough to be carving out this collection of what I consider to be rules for anyone, beginner or intermediate or even experts, who want to see more success in the stock market.

I am no famous personality, not a television worthy fund manager nor one of the numerous trading gurus that you can find a dime a dozen these days. You can try googling for me, but chances are you won't be finding much. I term myself as the man on the street investor cum trader. No silver spoon nor special circumstances marked my gradual accumulation of wealth primarily gotten from the stock market. I want you to know this because this means that you can also go out and do what I have done. You can possibly build your retirement fund yourself, give yourself bigger bonuses than what your current boss is giving you, and even become your own boss. I say all these not as words of motivation, but as words of fact. Of course, it will not be that easy. Anything worth having is never that easy, yet what I want to try doing with this book is to make your road just that bit easier.

You can be a complete beginner, just like I was back in high school. Or you can be already well familiar with the Dow Jones and S&P as well as the Russell 2000. This book will act as a guide book for those who are fresh starters and new to the game. It will also serve as timely, constant reminders to those who already have skin in the game.

I made the effort to write this not because of the want for fame or fortune, but because I was primarily thinking of how I wanted to help two of my friends out. One had come to seek advice from me on investing. Being a complete newbie to this, he knew virtually nothing about the financial markets and its myriad of instruments. Another also came to me, but this friend had tried his hand in the markets and gotten burned. Both of them wanted help so I thought this writing would serve to help them out with much better clarity than just conversation alone.

One word of caution however, this is no holy grail. Anyone who sells you the idea that there can be a be all and end all kind of answer to making money to the stock market should be placed high on your alert list. You can still listen on, as I have, but you need to know when you are being taken for a ride, and jump off that bandwagon before you get scammed of money and time.

Think about the Madoff pyramid scheme and countless other human inventions that prey upon the human emotions of greed and fear. Investing money with someone who promises you astronomical returns while having a hard time giving you the exact way of how he goes about doing it is really simply throwing your money down the drain. Buying this or that automated system and blindly following what the system churns out is also another way of trying to get out of the work that needs to be done. Think about it, when a farmer wants to reap a bountiful harvest, he must definitely plough the fields, sow the seeds and also have the patience to wait. The same goes for you if you wish to become a capable investor in the markets. There will be automated tools which will help us in the journey, but they should just remain as tools, not become the decision maker. You should always hold the final say. That is the reason why practical knowledge is so important in this field. I say practical knowledge because you can definitely read up on all the books surrounding the great legends like Warren Buffett and Peter Lynch, and yet still end up not doing much because you simply do not know how or what to do.

My aim is to allow you the chance to take the wheel in your own hands, and direct your ship in this veritable ocean of financial information. You definitely will not learn all that you need to learn, it would be foolhardy of me to make this claim, but you can be assured that after going through this, you will definitely have the knowledge to make smarter decisions for yourself with regard to gaining wealth in the financial markets. This book does not promise that you can make x amount of money in y number of days like what some other books do. That again would be foolhardy of me to make such a claim, and I do not do foolhardy things.

What I can promise you though, is that the knowledge and information found therein will stand you in good stead whether you are just a beginner, or someone trying to find more success in the stock market. I have shaped the information into what I would like to think of as rules. These are rules which should always define how you approach any investment or trading instrument. At the end of the day, always know this. You are the sole decision maker in the growing of your wealth, and all you should be doing is to gain knowledge and know-how to make that decision making process more robust and smooth. That sounds way different from the easier route of buying a system or relying on another person to make money for you isn't it? It is worth it though, because after all that training and perseverance, you gain something that no one can take away from you.

In the end, a lot of what happens next in your investing and wealth accumulation journey will depend primarily on you. I would like this opportunity to be present during this time in the form of these rules which I have collated from my years of investing and trading so that they might be of some help to you. Read them, peruse them and most importantly, think about them, because sometimes deep reflection may yield unexpected answers.

I would like to take this chance to say this in honesty. You have made a correct choice in wanting to learn how to grow your wealth through the stock and financial markets. In this day and age, it is my humble opinion that having a job is no longer a sure fire way to securing a steady retirement. One must always have multiple streams of income if it were possible. Embarking on this learning about making money from the stock market is but another avenue for you to broaden your income streams so that you become more diversified and not so reliant on your day job. For this, I am happy for you, because you have already taken a positive step by taking in the knowledge presented within this book.

Let's get on with it!

CHAPTER 1

Rule Number One (Don't Leave Home Without Doing It)

---○---

This is rule one, so in my book it is one of the most basic of things. Something similar to taking a breath or maybe munching on your food. This is something basic, not the most important but a staple in your arsenal of how-tos when it comes to dealing in the financial markets or anything for that matter.

Knowing What You Are Getting Into

That is right. This is the number one rule. Always know what you are getting yourself into, before you even take one step in that direction. You always want to know what is hiding at the end of the rainbow, as the pot of gold may be booby trapped or worse still non-existent. Just ask those folks who partook in lucrative sounding projects which later showed themselves to be nothing more than well-dressed pyramid schemes.

This makes it important for you to know not just the general idea of how things work, but it is also helpful to have some inkling of the technical knowledge contained within as well. At the end of the day, whether you are investing or trading in stocks, forex, futures or cryptocurrencies, the basic requirement is always to understand the product, so that you can undertake the decision on when to buy and sell that much better.

Basics Of The Stock Market

Let us know peer into what the stock market is. At its basest form, owning a stock is not much more than owning a piece of company where the stock originated from. You become a holder of equity when you buy into a stock. This generically means that you will do well if the prospects of the company does well. Similarly, if the company takes a down turn, then your stock value will then probably depreciate.

Many folks find this easy to grasp, while others still think that the stock market is just a screen or a website which shows ticking jumping numbers. Behind those ticking jumping numbers are actual companies present in everyday life. This gives us an insight to one of the ways of investing in the stock market. You will realize or discover many things if you just stop and ponder a little deeper for a bit. Everyone loves to have the example of Apple stock, but maybe a lesser known name like

Keurig Dr Pepper may draw a bit of your attention. This stock is what most investment folks term as a consumer staple stock. When you break down that $50 dollar word, consumer means folks like you and I, while staple means you really can't do without it for any extended period of time. Things like foodstuff, drinks, as well cleaning items will come into mind when we talk about this. Key to this is also the fact that staples tend to get purchased consistently. If you looooove doughnuts, and Krispy Kreme is one of your top choices, you just might have known about Keurig if you thought about it and dug a little deeper.

What I am getting at is this. There are many stocks out there, as there are many investment opportunities. Not all of these money making stocks are known only to the top analysts and hot shot investors. Many have household brands in their stables and we just have to dig a little deeper into the things we use, the things we like, and we just might be able to find a potential winner.

Beyond knowing that a stock is essentially a piece of a company, we have also got to know some of the technical bits which I mentioned earlier. The stock counter or the ticker is the representation of the company in the stock market. Whenever you want to buy or sell a stock, that is one of the most crucial things you need to inform your broker.

Volume

There is then volume, which shows the total quantity of stocks that exchanged hands on a daily basis. Volume is an important tool that many fundamental and technical analysts will use. It also forms a crucial leg of the technical analysis method called Price Volume Analysis. Volume speaks of the commitment of the market to the stock. A higher price and a low volume weighted against a higher price and high volume does give differing signals as to how the stock will turn out.

Price

Price is another key component. In most cases you have to be familiar with the bid and ask price. Bid price is what you can sell your stock at, while Ask price is what you can buy your stock at. The difference between the bid and ask will be called the bid-ask spread. This spread is there so that technically there can be no instant buying and selling of the stock just to spike up the volume. Always take note of the bid ask spread if you are seeking to trade the market. If you motive is a little more long term though, the spread will have lesser immediate consequence.

There is also the other portions of the price which you need to pay attention to and these would be the open, close, highest and lowest price for the day. The open price is what the stock has started the day at. It is not always the case where it would start off from where it left off the previous day. News, announcements and various other factors can cause the price to open higher or lower than that of the previous day. This is what we call gap ups or gap downs. The closing price of the day would essentially be the stock price at the end of the trading session. Many folks would like to use the closing price as a very short term barometer on the health of the stock. A higher close against the open shows positivity, while the reverse bodes ill news. For the highest and lowest prices, these are used by investors to gauge the extremes of the price movement for the stock. In other technical analysis courses, the use of Japanese candlesticks as well as bar charts incorporate these price points very well, and there are such things call candlestick charting courses which purport to teach the ability to predict price movements of the stock. All things being fair, I have been through this stage too when I grasped at whichever course that could just unlock the secret to the riches of the stock market for me. What I learnt is that there is no short cut to hard work, and my personal note on Japanese candlesticks is that I absolutely love to use them when I am doing my technical charting. I like the presentation and how they easily show the open, close, high and low of the stock price. However,

I do not lend weight to the idea that you can make constant long term wealth just by using candlestick and candlestick patterns alone.

Year High and Low

This is what many would know as the 52 week high and 52 week low prices. Most folks just term it as year high and low but in actual fact, it is a rolling 52 week price point, so to term it simply as year high or low is a bit off the mark here. The impact of such price points are not to be scoffed at. When a stock breaches it 52 week high or low, many would sense blood and with a right confluence of factors, the price can move by a large margin. However, to just senselessly base a whole trading strategy on looking at the 52 week high and low would leave just about any one open to disastrous setbacks.

Dividend Yield

This is of most interest to many passive investors out there who just like to sit back and watch their stocks generate cash for them annually. Not a bad position to be in I must really admit, and one which I find myself currently in. However, as someone who has also been on the other side of the fence as well, I know full well that in order to amass capital that is capable of generating retirement levels of dividends, is no small thing indeed. The dividend yield is basically the dividend divided by the current price of the stock. Dividends are paid on a semiannual or annual basis, so to get the yield is also to know an approximate time when you can break even on the purchase of that particular stock. The caveat here is all things being constant, which means you have to assume that the dividend payouts do not change. So for a stock that has a dividend yield of 5%, that effectively gives the buyer a 20 year time line to break even on the stock, leaving aside capital gains and having the condition of constant, unchanging dividends. This is a good metric to look at for assessing the health of the company, but as always, making decisions based on just dividend yields alone just doesn't cut it.

Leverage

This here is the veritable double edged sword. When we talk about leverage, we are talking about buying shares using money which we do not have. Most investors purchase their stock and pay it up in full. They own the stock and it is clean cut. For folks who purchase their stock using margin, they put down a deposit and they would have to maintain a positive balance in order for them to keep that position. Should the stock price move against them, they would be required to top up that balance, else the position would be closed and they end up not owning any stock on top of making losses. Many folks who trade on margin do not see that, because they can only fathom the fact that they will be making their money work harder for them using this form of leverage. When they just have to pay up the deposits in order to get positions in their preferred stocks, their usual rationale is they can get probably 2 or 3 positions instead of just one should they opt against just paying it in full. That makes sense, but it is also crucial that we take note of what can happen if things go south.

Similarly, we are talking about leverage when we look at contracts for difference (CFDs). These are in fact derivatives of stocks, which means at the end of the day, they are just meaningless pieces of paper contracts which do not allow any company ownership unlike the actual stocks. Folks use CFDs for the pretty much the same reasons. They want to get rich using as little money as possible. That comes at a price though. On top of having to maintain a positive balance in order to keep your CFD positions, CFDs charge interest to their users depending on their type of positions. A position where you buy is known as long, while a position where you sell is known as short.

Long positions tend to attract lower interest when compared to short positions but they attract interest all the same. That means that for every day of maintaining that CFD position, you are actually bleeding money if everything stays put. One important thing to note however, is that CFDs give investors the option of shorting or short selling. This is effectively a situation where you sell stocks which you do not own and wait to buy them back later at a lower price, thereby making money if you think the stock price is going to tank. Short selling using normal stocks is a trifle more difficult, and really depends on your broker. Some brokers do not allow short selling while others only offer limited stocks which they can short sell. Short selling using CFDs however, is primarily seamless because the CFD is essentially a contract between you and the broker. There is no actual stock in the picture and all you are concerned with is the stock price. This ability to take advantage of a bearish or price dropping market, is the reason why some folks choose to take the risk. I myself have done this many times, but like I said earlier, it is a double edged sword. So it is imperative that we are clear with how utilization of this particular form of leverage can hurt or help us, then we can make decisions about it with much more clarity and conviction.

The Act Of Buying And Selling Stocks

This is again one of the crucial pillars in your journey to amassing stock market riches. The act of buying and the act of selling of stocks. Technically, it all involves the brokerages and they will be the ones who would be executing your orders for you. These days, most retail investors would be doing their transactions via the web through the brokerage portals or apps. There are some minority who still wish to speak to a human broker though, in order to get that perceived sense of affirmation before making the final call.

For me, I always do orders myself. This is to cut cost as having a human broker handle your transactions would involve higher transactional fees most of the time. That's the core reason why I like to handle stuff myself. Another thing to note is that when you handle your own execution, you actually get to see the price movements nearer and up close. Some may argue against that, while others would vouch that you can never do without it. To me, I just like to be near where the action is. Just like how a restaurant operated by a real chef who knows how to cook is infinitely better than a restaurant employing their chefs, you would want to have real time practical knowledge of the execution side of things. This boils back to my take on having knowledge on the stuff that you are going to get into. This way, you know what you do not know, and more importantly what you do know, thereby having a lesser chance of getting wool pulled over your eyes.

I will not be recommending any brokerages over here though. Everyone has their own preferences, and it would be presumptuous of me to think that my choices are always right. What I can say though, are the things to look out for when searching for a competent broker. First thing of course is to make sure that your brokerage is fairly licenced and able to operate in your country's jurisdiction. No point dealing with bucket shops in a bid to cut fees and then having your funds disappear into thin air when the bucket shops mysteriously disappear.

Next would be looking at the kind of orders you can get from the brokers. Many brokers these days offer more than just the standard buy and sell orders. Amidst the myriad of different orders, two of the most important orders in my opinion would be the stop and limit orders. Both buy and sell sides will have stop and limit variations, so there will be buy and sell stop orders, as well as buy and sell limit orders. To illustrate it, say a stock has a current price of $10. A buy limit order would be placed below the $10 because a limit order has to be executed at a more favorable price as compared to the current one. So in this example it could be a buy limit of $8. When the stock price drops to $8, the buy limit is converted to a standard or market buy order, and you get your stock at $8. A sell limit would be the reverse, with it being placed say at $15, because like I said, a sell limit order needs to be executed at a more favorable price than the current. So when you are placing a sell limit order at $15, you would be wanting to sell the stock when it bounces up to $15 from its current $10 mark.

A sell and buy stop on the other hand would be something of a reverse. In a sell stop order, you would place it at $8, below the current $10, and when it hits $8, the sell stop becomes a market sell order and you will sell the stock at $8. People do this when they want to get out of a stock before they make too much of a loss. For the buy stop order, you would place it at $15 and then when the price moves from $10 to $15, your buy stop order will be triggered as a market buy order and you would be a proud owner of the stock at $15. Wait! What? Why would I want to buy a stock at a higher price? This brings us back to the talk about the 52 week high. Some folks actually buy the stock when it breaches the 52 week high point. That is where their buy stop order will be placed. Their rationale would be to take advantage of the psychological rush that the breach of the 52 week high would entail. Again I know it sounds old, but just purely basing any strategy on such simplistic thinking would probably not get you far.

I would like my broker to have such orders available to me at the minimum. Next up to think about would be the availability of CFDs from the brokerage. I know that it is a double edged sword, but the key is I would like to have that sword nonetheless. CFDs are a good way to short the market if you hold a bearish view of it. Of course I am not telling you to make use of that facility the moment you start investing. It is more of ensuring your broker has that facility in the event you truly want to use it.

The other thing I want to examine would be the bid ask spread for different stocks. Most of the time, major stocks that are in the Dow

Jones Index would have similar bid ask spreads across brokers, so the key here is to look at smaller stocks or companies to see if the spread is a bit too much. Bid ask spreads can make or break a trader, and it is also good to have a tight spread when you are operating as an investor too. I mean, every dollar saved can go towards building your capital for further investment right?

Markets And Indices

This portion here is another important pillar which you need to know. There are numerous markets besides the famous New York Stock Exchange (NYSE) which you probably would have at least heard about. The next prominent exchange would be NASDAQ, dealing predominantly with tech stocks. Besides these exchanges, IEX and the Chicago Stock Exchange are also the smaller exchanges present in the US. The majority of your action will be found between the NYSE and NASDAQ. These two exchanges combined hold most of the liquidity and stock counters in the country. That is not to say we do not need to pay attention to the smaller exchanges, but just that our major focus will be on the above two. Beyond US shores, every major country would have their individual stock exchange where their companies get listed and transactions take place. We will need to concern ourselves with them as your capital grows larger and you seek to find better investment opportunities outside of the US. Sometimes, when you are of the view that the US markets are overbought, it could be wise to cast your net elsewhere, perhaps in Europe or even Asia in order to maximize profit potential.

The next thing we want to look at would be stock indices. These would involve names like the Dow Jones Industrial Average, S&P 500, Russell 2000, DAX, FTSE 100 or Footsie as it is known colloquially, Nikkei 225 as well as the Hang Seng Index. They should not be confused with markets but instead you will know them as collections of stocks that are bundled together in order to reflect certain economic situations and to act as barometers. The Dow Jones Index or DJ has been used as such to determine the state of economic health in the US. Its 30 stocks can be chopped and changed so that it can better reflect the current situation of dominant companies.

In the past, it the DJ was dominated by steel stocks because they had a huge role to play in the building of rail and industrial expansion. These days, other tech companies are added into the index to better reflect the current economic conditions. The S&P 500 is another useful barometer to take note of when we want to gauge the health of the overall stock market. Weighing in at five hundred stocks , it has a broader representation of the market and hence some folks would think it is a better thermometer to gauge the economic temperature.

For me these indices are useful tools to see overall large trends and health. You can also trade them indirectly using futures or CFDs but there is no physical way for you to actually own a piece of the index. The index is simply an amalgamation of stocks artificially put together. Some folks, like the big boys are able to create close approximations of the index by getting the correct proportions of the individual component stocks. Others just use the futures or CFDs or perhaps even use an index fund in order to initiate a position. When I straight out take positions in any of the indices, this means that I am overall fairly clear about my view of that particular market, and more importantly, I am not clear of which individual stock should be worthy of my investment. That in my view, is one of the reasons why you might want to invest in an index. Do not take this as an easy way out from individual stock selection though, because getting an index call right is much tougher than getting an individual stock call right in my opinion.

Alternative Markets And Instruments

I know this book is titled stock market investing for beginners, but it would be unworthy of me if I did not talk about these markets and instruments in order to let you know what lies in tandem with the stock markets within the financial universe. This is because the rules that you will learn within this book will also stand you in good stead when you apply them to the other financial instruments as well. Another thing would be just that these markets also give you added opportunities for you to add to your investment capital.

First off, we talk about the foreign exchange market or forex market. This market is one of the biggest, dwarfing the stock markets by many fold. Logically it is not hard to see why. The biggest users of the forex market are companies and sovereign countries, when they trade internationally and hence have the need for currency exchange. This market is traded primarily using derivatives like futures where movements in the foreign exchange rate would determine profit and loss. Typically, when one of the currencies involved in the exchange is the US dollar, these forex pairs are called majors. For forex pairs that involve other currencies like the Norwegian or Swedish kronor, they are usually termed as exotics or minors.

The forex market is used primarily in a trading capacity for me, though it is also possible to have a long term investment angle on it. Forex pairs also pay out interest, dependent on difference in the two countries' prevailing interest rates. If there is interest paid out to you, it is known as positive swap, while a negative swap would mean that you actually lose interest when you are holding a position in that particular forex pair.

The forex market is also a close approximation to the bond market. This is because bonds are denominated in currencies and the currency exchange rates would fluctuate in response to how the bond markets are moving. In this respect, it would be safe to say that should there be loads of interest and buying up of US dollar denominated bonds, usually the US dollar would strengthen against other currencies. What this gives us is another clue on how the stock market and its related stocks may perform. Why so? Bonds are actually collateral debt existing on national and company ledgers. Ascertaining the level of demand for these debt is another positive way of looking at the health of the company which we are interested in purchasing stock in. Always remember, it is always good to use whatever we have at our disposal to gain insightful knowledge

However, due to its immense size of the forex market, it is nigh impossible for any broker out there to be able to furnish a proper volume number like how it is done with stocks. Any broker that claims to be able to do so, I would advise that you stay a pole's length away from them, as these brokers would be known in the industry as trading against you. They accept your orders and then take an opposing position. This means that they never pass on the order to any of the larger banks for clearance, and they will have all the incentive in the world to flush you out of your position. The way they do so would be broadening the bid ask spread of the particular pair where you have a position in, especially in times when major news is expected. The study of the forex market is going to be a deeper one if you wish to engage in active trading. However, for information gathering purposes in order to make a better stock selection call, knowing what to look out for would be more than sufficient to back up your knowledge arsenal.

The other market which you have to take note of would be the commodities market. This is the market where people will be talking about corn, soybeans, oil and gold. Typically traded in futures contracts, commodities form another market which can both provide information for better stock investment as well as being an outlet for potential capital investments.

When we talk about providing information, commodities have traditionally been the canary in the mine when it comes to economic health. The price of copper for instance, is a well-known barometer of world trade, simply because many items in the world need the metal for production. When copper price increases, you can see smiling faces on many investors' faces. Another example would be the price of gold. Gold is known as a safe haven. This precious, but fairly useless metal is perceived by humans to be of value infinitely, hence whenever there are threats of economic upheavals and worse, gold becomes in demand and its price correspondingly increases. Oil and coal prices would also serve the function of testing out the state of global economic growth as they represent energy prices.

Typically, commodities would probably not be your primary focus now at this point, simply because you do not have the luxury of actually owning the item that you are purchasing. True, it is possible to actually take delivery of the commodities contract when it matures but most futures contracts these days just close out the contract and tabulate the difference in profit and loss. Besides, when a single contract costs up to $250,000 without any leverage involved, that is a fairly significant outlay for any retail investor just for one position in a single commodity. Talk about putting your eggs in one basket!

We will use commodities more as information sources as well as trading avenues. It is still possible to hold investment positions in them but your capital would have to be a bit bigger in order to shave off quite a bit of the transaction costs. Next up we look at the new kid on the block. Cryptocurrencies.

Cryptocurrencies

This class of investment or speculative instrument has received loads and loads of attention since 2016, with its peak heightening in 2017 and then currently seeing a gradual normalization through 2018 and present time.

What are they exactly? Bitcoin, Litecoin and whole lots of other coins. Every corner you turn to seems to have something called ICO or initial coin offering. All promising to be the next big thing that will change the way global currencies work and maybe even take away certain aspects of business away from our good old banks.

The truth is, it is important to grasp the technology behind all these coins. That is the block chain technology. This piece of tech has the ability to empower every person who is in within the network to be able to have the ledger. If we come to think of banks and the enormous role they play in the financial markets, one of the key components is that they have the ability to be the central ledger. When your bank balance is stated as having a million dollars in the bank, that is what is regarded as truth. That is the reason why so many banks spend millions on cyber security, because if anyone were to hack into their system and change items on their central ledger, that would potentially cause loads of trouble.

With the block chain, everyone who is tapped into the network is then able to have the ability to be accountable for the ledger, because they all hold the ledger in a sense. Going back to the bank example, it is like all of us have become banks in our own rights, and anytime a transaction is keyed in the network, all of us banks will have our ledgers updated. Can you imagine the problems hackers would face if they tried to change each and every ledger?

That is the power of block chain technology and it would do everyone well to understand that better instead of being caught up with Bitcoin and the like. In fairness though, I would categorically state that the coins are by no means assets for investment, though I would not put it pass them to be suitable for trading or speculative instruments. Their volatility and movement in the market marks them suitable for trading but as longer term investment assets, I would really question what am I actually buying.

When you purchase a stock, you are buying into the future of the company. When you go long in commodities futures, you are being vested in that certain commodity. However, when you are buying bitcoin, though it would market itself to be the currency of the future, in reality it really is akin to a speculative stock that promises much but you may not know too much about how it can and will deliver. That is the reason why I would label it as trading ready but not for longer term investment.

For myself, I acknowledge the potential power of the block chain technology that is driving the crypto boom. So how would I actually get some skin in the game? My thoughts would be drawn towards companies which would actually benefit from these block chain technologies as they get more and more refined and user friendly. To me these are hedged bets. In the worst case scenario, I would be having companies which I know on my plate. In the event that things turn out as I would like, then these companies would benefit and they would realize synergies and economies of scale which would unlock and create more value in them.

Understand The Technicals Of The Game

I would like to stress again the importance of knowing what you are getting into whenever we talk about investing or trading. At the very least we should be familiar with the instruments and markets purely from a technical standpoint.

It is just like you learning to play golf or tennis. When you first start out, you would need to know the rules of the game even before you take your first swing. Imagine a tennis novice not knowing that there is a boundary on the tennis court, and all the serves being made land out of the court.

When you know the rules, then you can start to look at how you play, and to think of how you would want to play better. That would be covered in the later chapters, with the next one coming up to be intensely personal, so put your seat belt on and let's delve deeper into the arts of making money from stock market investing!

CHAPTER 2

Rule Number Two (Do This And Better Your Chances To Win)

There was an ancient strategist in China who once said "know yourself and know your enemies, and you will win all hundred battles that you engage in." The esteemed strategist was named Sun-Tze, and you might have heard of him. His teachings on warfare were considered to be paramount readings and in this modern day and age, they too have bearing on investing in the stock market. Especially the phrase above.

Know Yourself

Many folks just want to plunge straight into the market after reading this or that book that promises a system that generates a life time of passive income. Others can't hold their horses after learning about systems from seminars or webinars that need just one hour a day to make tons of cash from the financial markets.

In truth, I have also been amongst those folks. Trying my hand at this or that, only to realize that none of them work for me when I am so easily swayed by the market price movements. It can really seem like something of a curse at times. When you buy a counter, it goes down immediately by several points and your heart is in your mouth. It stays around that price point, tormenting you and giving you nightmares of plunging straight down even more. You cannot take it and sell off the stock, turning a paper loss into a real one. Within a day or sometimes within minutes, the stock turns on its head and bursts straight up. It would have netted a handsome profit had you not sold it just. You just blame it on your bad luck.

Now imagine the same scenario, where you bought the stock and it still plunged down several points. However this time, you are not really concerned about the drop, because you have worked out in your head what was the worst case scenario for yourself and also why are you actually initiating a long position in that particular stock. A movement of some points would not shake you. You don't bother about the price drop and after some time, the stock rebounds and bursts upwards, netting the same handsome profit for yourself.

At this juncture, you might be tempted to ask, what is the key difference in the above two situations? The answer is YOU. You are the crucial difference. Only when you have figured out your own mind and how it works in response to the market would you then be able to have a steadier presence and not be worried as much by price movements.

I know, it sounds easier said than done. I really do, because I have been through that as well. When you are handling investments and trades in which seem to be putting too much fear into your psychology, then you really are in above your head.

The crux of the matter now is, how do you settle yourself down and really know yourself when it comes to the markets?

Trading And Investing Psychology

Many people think they truly know themselves but they would be in for a bit of a shock when the clear mirror of the stock market is reflected back on us. The market never lies and it has no time for egos and false perceptions. One can bluster and brag for all they want, but if they shake and shiver in front of the stock market, their game is up and you would know their facades have fallen off.

For myself, I got out of this mire when I took a long hard look at who I really am. Some of the questions I asked myself were:

- What have I really got to lose if I were to continue investing and trading in the financial markets?

- What is it that is making me really scared and worried whenever things do not go my way after initiating trades?
- Why am I feeling so happy and invincible after a series of good trades and handsome profits?
- What do I want to get out of this investment and these trades?

Only when I had honest answers to these questions and more, could I really settle down and start turning around my investing and trading career.

The most important aspect of knowing oneself when it comes to trading and investing would be the question of "what do you have to lose?"

Let's have a thought about that. Imagine you have your last ten thousand dollars. You decide you want to get rich quick and really hope to the gods or whoever is listening in that the stock counter tip which you gotten from a really reliable source turns out very well. You sink your last ten thousand into the stock and then you wait.

Because it is literally your last ten thousand, and because you sunk every penny into the stock, every price fluctuation brings about a nervous flutter in your heart. A drop of ten points or more brings a sickly, sinking feeling. In this case, what have you got to lose if the investment really goes south? You lose all of your last ten thousand dollars and most likely would be feeling really despondent about it.

We always want to know what we can lose, before we even think about what we can gain from the stock market. When we know with certainty of what our potential loss is, it would provide a degree of stability because we would have come to terms with it in our minds. That is one of the best things you can do for yourself.

Let us illustrate with this example. You have a business that is comfortably making you five thousand excess cash each month. You tend to save these monies for a rainy day in the bank. One day, you chance upon a good book on stock market investing and start to learn more about it. Building up your knowledge, you then decide to enter the market and have a go. You however read somewhere that you must always decide what you are willing or able to lose before you even invest or trade any stocks. That is the reason why you decided that you can afford to take out ten thousand dollars for this journey into the investment realm. It is after all two months of excess cash from the business, so even if you were to lose it all, the damage to your personal circumstances would not be that great.

We can also look at the previous example of the bloke who had his last ten thousand dollars left in the pocket. If he had done some thinking, he might still be able to invest. How? Well if I were him, I might split the ten thousand into two portions. One portion is to save me from desperate circumstances while the other is dedicated to investment and trading. While there is the knowledge that it is still my last ten thousand dollars, I have actually made a sort of pact with myself that the portion dedicated to investments and trading would be something which I am willing to lose. If he were to lose it all, he still has his other portion to sustain him through life and perhaps get some sort of job and all.

Take the time to think through what is it you are willing to lose before taking the first steps into the markets. When you have a clear idea of what it is that you are willing to lose, then you have got to come to terms with it honestly.

Only after truly coming to terms with the potential loss, will you have gained a steadying rock with which to face the stormy, rocking seas of the markets.

I know it may sound counter intuitive to talk about losses and losing even before you have begun your stock market investing journey but trust me, it will be to your benefit if you were to take this seriously. Everyone out there is wanting to harp on the easy and quick ways to reap rewards from the markets without putting in much efforts because they have systems to sell and techniques to teach. No one will really talk about prepping your mind for what lies ahead.

This mind prep is really quite important because it will determine how you react and think when the markets move for and against you.

Tailor Your Actions Accordingly

When you know yourself, which means a bit more than the key of knowing what you can lose, then you are able to react and take appropriate actions.

When you know how much you can lose, the fear is lessened somewhat as you always have a voice in the back of your head saying this is the maximum amount you are going to lose, and you have been prepared for it, so no worries.

When we buy into a stock with no leverage used, the amount we place in to initiate the long position is literally the amount we lose if the company is run to the ground and goes bust. When we have mentally come to terms with that, it gives us relative freedom from shocks and fears and nightmares.

When you know how you would react when you have a little or some profit, then you can tailor your reactions. If you find yourself consistently being worried about the paper profits being eroded away by the market, then you would have to dig deeper to find out about your fears. Why would you be concerned with just a five point gain, when the profit potential is likely to be fifty points? The answer is could be stemming from the loss angle, where the person has not really come to terms with what he can lose, so he is wanting to just take whatever meagre profits there are now. It could also mean that the investor has over committed the amount and is now feeling uncomfortable about the size of the stock holdings in his portfolio.

It could also be a situation where the investor did not do the homework on the stock properly or had entered a long position on the basis of hearsay or tips, hence the worries present themselves when there is but a small profit. This happens because the investor does not really know what kind of profit he can expect or the profit potential of the company, hence the hurry scurry feeling will come with small profits.

Another aspect of things would be delving into the personality of the investor or trader and tailoring the investing approach in accordance with that. When the personality is one where one is eager for fast and quick conclusions, with not much of a patience for the drawn out wait, then it might be better for this person to focus more on shorter term trades rather than mid to long term ones. This person might take to day trading or swing trading that lasts no more than three days. It could even be a rule that he sets himself since he is familiar with how he feels. He could state that he would not hold any position for longer than two days because of his penchant for quick conclusions.

Another personality who has more of a patient approach, or a dislike for the quick and ever changing numbers that rattle the markets daily, may opt for a longer term approach in their investment horizon. It can range from weeks to months or even years if the investor has the stomach for it.

For myself, I tend toward the middle, where I vary holding positions between weeks and months because I found that I prefer the lifestyle that goes with this kind of trading. Day trading and scalping have been part of my repertoire before but I really did not enjoy sitting down for hours on end looking at figures jumping up and down. It is really a personal preference at the end of the day. Some folks I know get a huge buzz from day trading and making thousands in the day, and go to sleep in the night knowing they have zero positions in any stock. That is also the appeal of many day trading systems out there, yet they do not tell of the pressure and stress of having to make trades when there are not really any good ones out there because a day trader who does not make any trades does not make any money. Of course, there are also some select folks, who day trade, yet they do not have the pressure to trade daily because their earnings from one good trade could be in the millions. These folk would appear to have it all then? Yet they also have got to have the stomach to risk millions each trade. This means they have the preparation to lose millions in order to earn millions. Not everyone can do that.

The key here is to get a good grasp of yourself when you are investing and trading. You might want to start a journal to document down your feelings and emotional states. Most folks I know would recommend starting a trade journal, which is something that documents each and every trade that you do so that it becomes like a report card. For me I also include the psychological aspect of it as well in the trade journal. How I feel when I enter a trade, and how I feel during and when I exit the trade. Beyond that, you might want to consider keeping a feelings journal separate from the trade journal. This feelings journal will be used to document your emotional states during the course of your trading and investment journal.

If you are a day trader who trades from the market open to close, you would then document your feelings throughout that period. If you are a swing trader who take positions for weeks and work daily on your research and analysis of stocks, then you would document your feelings on a daily basis when you are trading and also analyzing the stocks.

Over time, you would be able to see patterns emerging that may be helpful in piecing together what your trading psychology is really like.

Before doing this personally, I had always been enamoured with the day trading lifestyle because I just thought it was very cool and efficient too! Little did I know my trading psychology was actually the reverse of this and that led me to better and better results in the trading and investing realm. Now, I am not saying that folks like me cannot day trade or do short term trades. We can, it is just that when you know you do something else better and with seemingly less effort, why would you want to pursue the more arduous way? The same could be said for the folks who have the natural capacity to day trade. They can take long term positions too, but the discomfort they may feel would outweigh the potential gains.

Build Up Immunity To Market Noise

Market noise is what we refer mostly to as the ups and downs of the financial markets. It can be new reports, price movements and just about anything which you may perceive as having a potential impact on the price of the stock you are currently vested in.

Noise in any case is mostly uncalled for in my opinion and it would be good to build up to a state where such noise will have as little impact on your decision making as possible,

Imagine you deciding to take a position and some well-meaning broker friend calls you and happen to chat about that particular stock. He intimates that it might be in for a fall according to his sources, and so you turn your long position into a potentially short one. How a decision can turn on its head in a split second! This kind of decision making should not be confused with decisiveness.

In decisiveness, you reach a well thought out decision that is backed by the careful and relevant accumulation of facts and numbers. When you flip flop like what happened above, that is merely having a change of heart because the initial decision wasn't grounded on solid facts in the first place.

How to accumulate and gather relevant information will of course be part of later studies, but it is most important for everyone to realize now that the ability to shut out market noise will only do yourself good and very little harm. You will save yourself much dithering and worries and this in turn will ensure that opportunities will be better taken while dangerous calls can be avoided.

Being able to shut out market noise also contributes to your peace of mind. Most of the financial programs and websites these days need a spin and angle on their stories in order to sensationalize and enable it to sell to the masses. As such, some or quite a bit of the news may not be what it really is. Whenever I think of this, I will always draw inspiration to a trader who traded from a log cabin in the hills. He only relied on a weekly news bulletin which reported the stock prices. It was said that he gotten all he wanted to know from the price movements themselves and did not have to bother with news and such.

It may sound out of this world and all, but as you delve deeper into this stock investing journey, you may just find and see for yourself real life examples of the trader from the log cabin.

One of the more practical ways which I always encourage novice investors to do would be to do some paper trading. This usually means getting an account set up with any brokerage account and they will fund it with fake money for you to trade according to real time price changes in the stocks and other instruments.

What paper trading does is that it will give you a basic grasp of the brokerage's platform with which to execute trades and place orders. It may also give you a little insight into your emotions when you trade, though not as much as if you were to risk real hard earned cash. Think about it, fifty thousand in fake money or five thousand in real cash, which would cause you to worry more if we need to risk them in the markets?

Graduating from paper to real trading is always good. In this aspect I would always encourage folks to risk a small amount. Imagine if you had one hundred thousand to invest, the initial amount I would recommend for real trading would be no more than ten thousand. Folks who do very well in paper trading may see a different ball game when it comes to real trading. Emotions are much stronger for one, and the susceptibility to market noise is very much heightened. In this kind of situation, one would have to constantly fall back to the tried and tested method of fact gathering and analysis. The only safe way of beating the market noise would be to take responsibility and ground the stock call in solid facts. This way, you are able to understand very thoroughly which of your calls are somewhat speculative while others are very much grounded and safe. It is then your decision on which calls you wish to pursue.

I have to say though, I don't make safe calls all the time. This is because the risk return ratio for speculative calls are sometimes so attractive that I find it hard to pass up. Would you risk one dollar for the chance to get five bucks in return? Some might scoff at this but that is a 5 to 1 risk return ratio, which I will take any day if I feel the circumstances are right. At this point though, I would like to say that any one starting out should still train themselves rigorously with solid grounded calls.

This way you will be able to differentiate which is which and will have lesser cause for worries and sleepless nights.

Greed And Fear

Why do I make somewhat speculative calls then, when I can be doing safer calls? Greed is the answer. This is something which we all have to come to terms with. The avarice within us has to be first acknowledged, then harnessed and controlled to enable us to have a profitable journey in stock market investing.

Greed if left unchecked, will be the principal cause for you to stubbornly hold on to a hundred point gain in hopes of ten more but end up making a loss when the stock crumbles and makes a swift descent.

Greed will also be the principal cause for you to hold on to a losing position long pass the point of the amount which you are willing to lose or your mental stop loss. This will cause extra losses eventually, as well as a constant reminder that you did not stick to what you have originally planned.

The other key emotion which we also need to grapple with will be fear. Fear naturally arises whenever we risk something which we own on an outcome which is fraught with uncertainty and cloaked in the unknown.

Fear is the one key reason why we often take profit on three or five point gains when the original target was a fifty pointer or more. Fear befuddles and creates even more confusion and worries that somehow, the only way to get out of that state is to close out the position in order to regain some semblance of peace.

I felt that way too before, and did all those things as I listed above as well. You do get a moment of burden lifting, as I would like to call it, but then the guilt and self-remonstration will start almost in the next moment. On days when the stock price soars after you closed out the meagre gains position, frustration ensues.

How do you actually tame and harness these two powerful emotions? You must first acknowledge them. See them in action while you are trading real cash, albeit using a small portion of the total amount you are willing to risk. This is where your emotional journal will be very useful, because you will be able to see where greed and fear impacts and hits you the most. That is why complete honesty in the journal is of utmost importance. No one else will read it anyway if you don't wish for them to, so be totally honest.

When feeling fear upon trade entry, write on that and think through the root of fear. What is the root cause for you to be feeling fearful when entering a trade? Could it be inadequate preparation before the trade, which means your decision is not based on solid grounded facts? Or could it be something which you just heard that has otherwise shaken your belief in your own stock call?

When you have pinpointed the cause and acknowledged the fear, you will then be able to take rectifying measures to lessen such recurrences in the future. If you know that you placed the trade without proper analysis and it was more of a punt, don't beat yourself over it but take another look at the stock in question. This time do a proper analysis and then decide if the position should be kept open or not.

If you are fearful because of market noise, then relook at your carefully prepared analysis and then stick to it, because you have already a system which you can rely on and market noise will always be market noise.

Greed is also controlled in the same way, through the careful journaling of your emotions during your whole investing process. In some ways, I would consider greed to be a tougher emotion to handle than fear.

This is so because greed usually presents itself when the going is good, when your calls are going well and the future looks even brighter. Greed then manifests itself into quite a bit of future thinking, where it would not be uncommon for you to think about what you want to do with your paper profits. You would also be forecasting how much you would be reaping in a year if things continue in such a manner.

Another aspect of greed is to also encourage the feeling of invincibility in the stock market. Imagine that you made ten calls and all ten calls were impressively correct. You get this sense of puffed up invincibility that on your eleventh call, you triple your usual size of investment and in doing so, exceed the amount which you are comfortable in losing. Do you think of the potential of loss at this point? Most definitely not! That is the reason why your usual careful, adequate analysis will fail you and you will overextend the limit of which you are comfortable in losing.

Some folks I know engage in such a practice. After they have a predetermined string of wins, it can be any number, five, ten or fifteen, it all depends on oneself, they will then deliberately have a loss in order to break up the string of wins. Of course they do not lose a lot, sometimes it could be less than a hundred or so. This is to act as a real reminder to them that they are not infallible, and to be constantly adhering to what works for them and their own systems of investing in the stock market.

I was curious to know how they actually engineered the loss and one of these folk told me that when it reaches his "losing call", he would randomly choose a stock and just take a position, without any analysis or what not. Once it reaches his stop loss, he would get out of the position.

Another shared that he would call up his stockbroker and ask for a specific stock tip. The very first stock that the broker recommends, he would carry out the order and then as usual, once it hits his determined stop loss, he would exit the position too.

Most of the time this works to generate a losing trade, but on the off chance that the broker or the randomly chosen stock sees a profit rather than a loss, these guys would quickly close off the position as close to their original entry price as possible. The whole idea is for them to get grounded in the basics and not have the big headed idea that they are bigger than the market. When one has the thought that everything they touch turns to gold, it is time to hide the gold.

Some Stuff Which I Use

The above portions have been dealing a lot with psychology and emotions, which is correct as almost half the trading battle is won when you have a clear and concise grip on your own emotions.

Besides keeping the journals and doing scaled down real cash trading in the initial stages, I also personally do some of these things which I find help in the emotional aspect of things.

Mindfulness

Practicing to calm the mind down and be in a better position to really identify the root of emotions is a strong asset to have when you are dealing constantly in changing numbers and contradicting reports. This is something which you have to gradually build up but it does take constant, daily practice. Even just having a period where you can observe your breath for five or ten minutes uninterrupted will give you a sense of calm that would be of good benefit to you. As you practice, the length of time can be increased.

This will help with emotions as mindfulness really allows us to first identify the emotions and then helps us with acceptance and acknowledgement. When we identify and accept the emotions like greed and fear, it allows us more control over them and it should be helpful for our journey forward.

Reading

And no, I am not referring to financial journals and magazines. In fact, I actively steer clear of those. I read as widely as possible and as long as anything piques my interest, I will gladly take a dive into it.

The reason I do this is to give the mind a different perspective on things. Think about it, for much of the waking hours, you are quite immersed in the markets and numbers. This reading is to give the mind a break while at the same time capture potential relevant knowledge which you never know may come in useful in the future.

CHAPTER 3

Rule Number Three (Things Which You Want To Know)

This portion here will be covering something of the meat and gristle of things, or the thick of things to put it simply. We will be looking at the various different strategies which most folks would be using for their investments in stocks and other instruments, while at the same time looking at different schools of thought when it comes to investment analysis.

Remember, there are many many roads which lead to Rome. The market can be traded and invested in as many ways as there are human beings on earth. Every single one of us have our own quirks and particular fancies, so there would not be a one size fits all solution available.

Having said that, there are however principles which everyone can base their personal investment and trading systems upon, so as you go along, you will get to realize that trader A's system may be largely similar to investor B's formula, but they each have their own particular nuances which are catered to their specific needs.

Common Strategies You Will Always Hear About

Over here, we shall be talking about some of the more common strategies which many people would probably have heard off, even if they aren't really familiar with the workings of the stock market.

Buying On Down Days

This in theory is not a bad idea. The broker rings you up and tells you the market seems to be having a depressed day, and it might be a good idea to pick up some stocks on the cheap.

As you will have come to expect, there are always two sides to a coin when it comes to stock market investing.

If you are someone with a solid system for analyzing stocks and have based your investing decisions on solid facts and numbers, then a down day could indeed represent a time when you might wish to pick up some stocks which you have been targeting for a lower price. Further, a down day does not mean you expend all your resources on those lower priced stocks. More often than not, the astute investor would be pushing in the positions in portions, with the view that a down day could very well become a down week. That would mean better prices to pick up the stocks at.

If you are however, just banking purely on the broker's tips and calls, a splurge into the market on a down day could become a catalyst for sadness if the market doldrums extend into the week or even into a month. You just bought, thinking it was a good price, and now it has gone even lower.

Buying on down days should not be taken as a strategy on its own but as part of an overall well formulated system. There is however, an argument that buying on down days can indeed be a strategy, and it goes like this.

You purchase on a down day. If the price goes down further on the following day, you purchase double of what you have done. Then, if the price goes down further on the next day, you again double your purchases of the previous day. At this stage you would have already made seven multiples of the initial first day purchase.

You then continue this purchase if the down ward move continues, until there is a bounce where the price of the stock does not go below the previous day and then you sell off everything.

Because you have been accumulating stock in larger amounts at lower prices, you have effectively averaged down your cost and hence, when there is a price bounce, selling off everything should nett a profit.

The issue with this is the need to have vast amounts of resources in order to perpetuate the constant buying. Imagine this going on for fifteen days, how many multiples would that be? Not something that I would recommend, because the risk reward ratio to me is not worthwhile.

Dollar Cost Averaging

This is what many financial advisors as well as folks pushing the funds and exchange traded funds (ETFs) will actually recommend. The basic premise is that you determine a date, say the first day of the month to plunk in your cash into the financial instruments regardless of the price fluctuations on that day. You then do this consistently for the following months, with every first day of the month being the time chosen to push your money into investments.

You essentially take market timing out of the scenario, or actually randomize market timing. By injecting funds on that specific date and time every month, you disregard the pricing conditions at that point in time and just focus on having your positions met.

Financial advisors adore this model because it makes for easier management of the clientele's portfolio. Of course, dollar cost averaging also has its merits, under certain conditions. It is our job to know what those conditions are and how dollar cost averaging can be then played to our advantage.

Generally, when the market is trending upwards, having a fixed amount to invest on a certain date will ensure that you will be actually purchasing lesser units at a higher price.

The opposite will be true when the market is trending downwards, where the fixed amount will then trigger a larger quantity of purchase at a lower price.

The commercial appeal of dollar cost averaging to most folk would be the fact that it looks like an idiot proof way of investing. Think about it, you set aside a comfortable sum per month or per year or whichever time period you choose. Then you just plunk it into the stock or stocks you chose. More often than not though, you would push it into mutual funds or exchange traded funds because those are actually vehicles that are vested in multiple stocks and assets, and you then think it might be better for diversity and safety.

For me, if you want to invest in the stock market and its associated financial markets, timing can never be completely erased from the table. Why?

Folks who blissfully do dollar cost averaging for one whole year or even two or three years can see half or much of their investment value wiped out just because they happen to be investing in a bear market and their dominant strategy was to go long or purchase stocks.

If one were to really want to trade or invest like an ostrich, then the minimum horizon would need to be at least seven to fourteen years. This is so that you allow a full two economic cycles to present itself and thus have their corresponding impact on the financial markets.

To me, dollar cost averaging has its uses, but you must learn how to use it, and more importantly to decide if it is indeed suitable for your personal use. This kind of investment strategy would be great for folks who have infinite amounts of patience, have a good job or excess cash flow every month coming in, and don't really get bothered with the amounts they are ploughing into the markets. The crux is that they should be investing an amount which they are very much comfortable with, and that they will hardly ever need to touch that investment amount except in the direst of emergencies.

These folk will benefit well from this strategy, and it pretty much suits them because they probably do not have a crushing interest to study the stock markets even on a weekly basis. Their earnings, though comfortable, will find it extremely tough to surpass market timers. I am saying this in fairness and based on what I have seen and experienced. It is by no means knocking on the dollar cost averaging strategy. Like I mentioned earlier, multiple roads lead to Rome, and everyone has their preferred way to go.

Dollar cost averaging can indeed be looked upon as a stand-alone strategy, albeit a fairly simplistic one. Folks who wish to receive maximum benefits from it would still need to analyse and time the market though, while for those who just want to let their money work harder for them without going through the headaches, a longer holding period or horizon will then be warranted and needful.

Bear Market Strategy

This is actually a derivation of the buy on down days scenario. Bear markets are typically categorized as such when the market has seen a decline of twenty percent in price levels, or when the markets have undergone continued downward pressure for many months, sometimes even leading to years.

For me, bear markets may have multiple and differing technical yardsticks with which to determine them by, but a quite simple method is to go out to the streets and start talking to folks whom you are wont to meet daily. Cab drivers, waiters in the restaurants and maybe even the elementary school teacher! When none of them wish to speak to you about the stock market, you are probably in the money if you place your bet that the economy is probably in the doldrums and the market is fairly bearish.

When markets are bullish, every one becomes a stock market whiz and that is when the term irrational exuberance presents itself. Conversely, when no one wishes to offer their well-meant advice on which stocks to purchase or short, and when even the whisper of the stock market would send people into jitters or for them to warn you to stay away, then you probably know the bear market is well and truly on its way.

The bear market strategy is also quite simple. Just correctly identify the period of the bear market, and then what you need most is actually conviction. Because you will be going out into the market and purchasing stocks when most people are huddled at home with their cash stock piles.

Building up your conviction will mean having sound and solid analysis of the companies which pique your interest, while also ensuring you are not overstretching yourself in the resources department. Bear markets can be fairly short, while some can be fairly lengthy, so that is why the conviction to stay vested is important in order to realize the profit potential.

These kind of situations do not present themselves daily or weekly, so it would be safe to say that folks who are dealing with day trading or shorter term swing trading would not really have much to do here. The bear market strategy is more for those who are usually having cash on hand, and they have done their homework such that when the time comes, they are without hesitation and are able to act with confidence when everyone around them is backing away.

One quirk is that some may actually combine the dollar cost averaging technique with this bear market strategy. This requires the foresight and certainty that the bear market is indeed upon us, and then a simple plan can be crafted to initiate constant purchases of stocks and funds as the prices keep on dipping. Some prefer this as compared to having to sink in larger sums in one go while others prefer to stick to their analysis and base their purchases on price levels which they have calculated to be of value.

Again I would say, there is no right or wrong in both cases. Most importantly, the methodology must be a good fit for the investor. As

I would like to say, if you win a hundred thousand dollars but are constantly shivering with fear and drenched with sweat, I would rather profit ten thousand yet be sleeping peacefully and without any worries.

The bear market strategy has its place and time for utilization, but it is not suited for those looking for quick trades by its very nature of being a bear market. To me, it is a very very good opportunity for investing the excess funds which you have little use for, and are able to stay parked in stocks or instruments which potential may not reap rewards till some years down the road.

Day Trading

This used to be a fad when I was still coming to grips with the market. I reckon it still must be at this point in time. Most proponents of day trading would say that it is one of the best methods to trade and get rich. You enter and exit all your positions within the day. You scout and target your stocks within the day. You make all your decisions within the trading time frame and then when the market closes, you are a happy person because you can go to bed with no worries, unlike those who are having existing holdings.

All this is fine and dandy, but as I have always mentioned, anything with regards to the stock market will always have two sides to it.

When you lock yourself to only being able to trade within a day's time frame, what happens when you do not have any good trades to choose from? Do you think you would have the pressure of having to make a trade else you actually might not earn anything for the day? What happens if this kind of trade less situation occurs for more than a day, two days or even three days in a row? Can you imagine the stress and pressure the day trader must be facing at this juncture? To get out of this, the day trader may then be forced to go into a trade which might not be the most optimal. This represents an increased potential for loss.

The usual counter argument to this would be that the universe of stocks as well as financial instruments are so huge, there will surely be at least one good trading set up every day. The universe might be big, however the extent that you can comfortably do analysis on the stocks which you want to trade would be limited by your energies. Artificial intelligence and computerized aids can only do so much, with the human brain still needed for deeper analysis.

The other aspect that you have got to note about day trading would be on the profit side. Say you have day traded a stock. It went up twenty points in the day and you have happily banked in your profits. The next day, it gaps up, where the stock price just opens at a much higher price than the previous day's closing price. This kind of situation happens when there is positive overnight news or when the buying interest is so very strong.

As a day trader, you are forced onto the sidelines when this kind of upward rush happens. You might be tempted to get in on the act and just jump in disregarding your systems and rules, and that would be the first step to folly.

For me, day trading is more of an opportunistic art. We can practise it when there is an ideal window to do so. It is very much like how hunting and fishing used to be done – in seasons. When the season is ripe for day trading, we should be doing it because it does really improve your sharpness as well as adding to your profit potential. When the season is not present, we should have our other systems and methods with which to rely on. Day trading does not work all the time but when it can be put to use, it is another good tool in the arsenal.

One word of caution though, you probably have got to practise more to get the hang of day trading. This is due to its demands for speed as well as quick decision making, and also the need for precise analytical skills. Sometimes you might hear folks who say they trade from the gut or they just had a feeling that they got to get out of the stock. Take these with a pinch of salt and look more into it. These guys probably have had tons of experience dealing with the market or with that particular stock, which is why they are able to seemingly act on their whims and fancies. In actuality, their minds have processed whatever information they needed and hence they are able to make the decisions so quickly.

Shorting

This side of the game holds some mystery and allure to many folks because approximately 50% of people are still only conversant with the idea that stocks can be only bought. They do not grasp the notion that you can actually short sell stocks which you do not own, subject to brokerage terms and conditions of course.

Typically short selling would require that you short sell from a list of stocks that the brokerage has made available. This is because these are stocks which the brokerage owns or they have obtained permission from the stock owners to allow borrowing. Short sellers would then be able to sell the stocks they do not own, but would have to pay interest for every day in which their short positions are active. This same interest paying goes when we are also talking about contracts for difference. (CFDs)

Shorting as a strategy is again part of the overall game which you can add to your repertoire. Imagine the bear market scenario, where it is just the onset of the bear market. You know that the market probably has got room to drop 20% or more and if you have got the ability to short certain chosen stocks, why not make a profit on the way down before you make the turnaround and start collecting the stocks on the cheap?

Is it definitely needful that you have got to master shorting? I would say it is good to know and a good option to keep open, but it is not a must have in order to be successful in the stock markets.

Take the bear market scenario we talked about earlier. If you did not have the option or just did not fancy shorting, you would have just stayed out of the market until the bear market buying kicks in and you initiated your long positions in the stocks of your choice. What would you be doing in the meantime when the market was heading down you ask? You could be sitting happily on cash doing nothing, or you could be investing in other markets. Markets do not all move in tandem, and when one is in the beginning stages of a bearish cycle, another could be flowing into the start of a bull run.

One thing of note which I feel compelled to say would be that shorting tends to see faster profits in the short term. What do I exactly mean?

If you were to short a stock at a certain time and you got the call correct, the downward movement will usually be much swifter than if you were long the exact same stock with the same correct call. That is why profits from shorting usually arrive much faster than profits from longing.

This is stemming from the two major emotions, greed and fear. In the case of shorting, fear is the dominant emotion that can be seen in the stock market. When a stock is taking a tumble, most folks who are vested may be unable to take the shock and would want to get out soon. Their overarching thought would be not to lose any more of their money in that stock.

When we have a stock going up in price, greed is the principal factor because people are buying in and pushing the price up in hopes that they can sell it later for a higher price. Greed has a slightly lower motivating factor than fear because the human psyche always wants to protect what it has first. It cannot tolerate detaching anything it owns. That is why the fear of loss always trumps the greed of gain.

This is just something for you to take note, but it is by no means a clarion call for you to jump onto the shorting bandwagon. I reiterate, it is good to know but by no means is it a must have in order to do well in the stock markets.

Penny Stocks

I am not sure when this strategy actually came into dominant play but to be honest, I have never really consciously utilize it. This does not mean I have not taken positions in penny stocks, but it does mean I did not initiate those positions just because they were penny stocks.

This strategy focuses much on penny stocks, which are fairly cheap as compared to the more main stream stocks that are in play. You can get thousands or even tens of thousands of shares when you are taking a position in a penny stock. The whole idea would be to wait for some tick up in the price movement, and then by the dint of volume, you actually sell off the penny stock holdings to cash in some profits.

A variation of the penny stock strategy would be to look into a few sectors which you deem as bullish, and then enter positions into penny stocks which belong to those sectors. Your holdings per penny stock would not be massive this time round, because you would be hoping for a larger price movement to realize the profit potential.

My positions in penny stocks have always come about after I put the stock through analysis, and I most definitely did not have the criteria that the stock must first be a penny stock.

Penny stocks belong to that category for a reason, which can range from anything like the company being badly run, to larger systemic things like it being in a sunset industry. Growth and value are not to be seen hence the tumble in price to what is deemed as the penny level. Of course, on occasion the market could be badly wrong, or the penny stock company executes a marvellous turnaround.

Most of my deals in pennies revolve around the fact that the companies are still deemed to be of some value with potential for growth, and it is only due to transient factors which hammered the stock price down for it to qualify as a penny stock. When I say transient though, it could be either a short or long wait. We just never know.

As such, penny stock investment strategy is not really one that can hold water in my opinion if the system were just purely based on having the criteria of the stocks having to be penny stocks.

That smells too much of a gamble to me, and smacks too much of hope. Hoping that the stock would move up some day, or hoping for the price to just move so that the entire holdings could be sold for some profit. When you find yourself hoping in the stock market, and there is nothing else to justify your continued investment, then it should be about time to place the exit order.

Know Yourself

I know this has been said before, but I would like to say it again in the context of these commonly met investment strategies.

As we have seen, all the strategies have their uses. What is more important now is to get a good grasp of how your trading psychology is and then select those strategies which you reckon would be a good fit for yourself.

A person who is disliking having to look at the screen and being tied down to the desk all the time would be a poor fit for day trading. A person who likes constant action and lives for immediate gratification would be a poor fit for bear market strategy.

As it is, there is no one size fits all strategy out there. What is more logical would be to accumulate knowledge of differing strategies which you deem are suitable for yourself and then shaping it into a coherent system that can be easily used by yourself.

Having said that, I would like to qualify that these above common strategies mentioned so far are what I would consider to be the tip of the iceberg. We shall be discussing a little more in depth regarding the schools of investment analysis later on and that would really open up more into the world of investment strategy.

Strategy School Of Thought

This portion may elicit some intense argument. I am all prepared for it because I myself have been through trading via both schools of thought. This is the ever present debate on fundamental analysis versus technical analysis.

Before I go any further, I would like to point out the value of analysis in the stock picking world. The results of a well worked and stringent analysis is often a bedrock which can help to support your decision in times when everyone and everything is saying just the opposite of what you are doing. Analysis gives you conviction, and with conviction, you have the steadying power and the ability to ride out the rough waves and block out the market noise. More importantly, you develop your own perception and point of view regarding the stock and the market. That is always invaluable. Even if you may be wrong, but the very idea that you have formed a view based on a stringent and well worked system gives you the ability to fine tune and adjust your view points with respect to the market as your journey goes.

Think for a bit in the shoes of someone who does not have a view. He instead relies on news reports, stock magazines and his brokers to feed him with ideas on what should be his next big investment. Compare that with someone who is trained to have a perception and angle on the markets. True, he may still get news and brokerage reports, and who's to say he cannot draw inspiration from these material to hit upon a good stock call? The key difference is in the fact that the trained person will do his own checking and stringent analysis in order to form his point of view. He can then compare his perception with those presented in the material. If there is obvious divergence, then he can easily let it go.

This is in contrast with the person who does not have a view. If he lets the call go, he would be worried about feeling regretful if the stock does indeed soar to the moon. Yet, he is also traumatized with every price fluctuation even if he is vested in the stock because he lacks conviction.

Fundamental and technical analysis proponents have been at loggerheads for as long as anyone can remember. Each side firmly believes that their school of thought is the superior one and thus encourage folks to take up studies in either direction.

For myself, I should venture to say that my formal education was in the area of fundamental analysis. That means I was schooled in the arithmetic of the company balance sheet and cash flow statements. We learned to look at the company and to ascertain its value such that we might be able to forecast the direction of the stock price.

It was fun in school, because the numbers are fairly stagnant and you did not have to contend with emotions or the hustle and bustle of the financial markets. Assumptions made on paper remained constant and did not change. Business conditions were also not thoroughly factored in. You did not have instances of malpractice or unethical behavior that would negatively impact the stock price. All in all it was pretty clean and sterile.

Folks who firmly believe in fundamental analysis believe in the fact that the income, cash flow statements as well as the balance sheet presented in the annual reports are the main piece of the puzzle which they would use to crack the code of the market. They are also of the predominant thought where they treat stocks as purely businesses, and hence their thought process would revolve around assessment of the business landscape and such like. Industry prospects and barriers to entry would near the top of their considerations whenever the decision to buy or sell a stock takes place.

For me, fundamentalist do very well when they operate in the longer term scheme of things. The analytical bent of looking at the fundamentals of a company will lead you toward a filtration process. You would be able to weed out the truly strong from the apparent ones, while at the same instance, you would be able to also filter those which aren't that seemingly weak as what the market seems to dictate.

As a fundamentalist, we are able to sniff out the good companies, and barring any unforeseen circumstances like insider manipulation or corruption, the only thing is to wait for the market to align with our expectations of the chosen company.

That is also the problem.

Sometimes, it takes a little time before the market catches on, and you would be able to reap your just rewards for having made a correct pick. Other times, it may take years or eons to you. You happily went in with the investment and expected some rewards within a certain period of time, and yet those expectations fell flat. The market just does not seem to see what you can see so plainly! During this while, your investment lies stagnant, and the monies locked up, unable to be deployed elsewhere for better profit potential.

In a world where there was someone with unlimited resources, I reckon he would be a very happy fundamentalist, as he would be able to park funds in those companies he ascertained as well worth the investment and then just wait for the time to ripen. He would have no worries with the opportunity cost of funds because he has virtually unlimited resources. That is of course the ideal world. We live in the real world, so we will have limited resources to call our own.

At this juncture, this is where technical analysts come in to point out the apparent flaws of the fundamental school of thought and then delight in their apparent advantages of the pure technical trading system.

Technical trading for me represented the holy grail at one point in my life, I was so fixated with it because I truly believed that if I just but find the correct technical system, my life would be set and my trading career would just be an easy one.

Many sellers of technical systems out there also seek to answer those expectations that having "the" technical system would represent wealth and passive income for pretty much the rest of eternity.

Take it from me, there is no such thing as a holy grail in trading. Pure technical systems may do well in certain periods yet return all the profits and make double the losses in other periods. Trading algorithms may see returns in certain windows, yet give nothing but losses in others.

This is not to burst your bubble but telling the truth as what it is. For all those folks who just say that they solely believe in the power of their moving averages, candle stick patterns and Fibonacci retracements, you can be pretty sure there should be more than meets the eye.

When I was first starting out with learning technical trading, I was like an energizer bunny. Back testing was the name of the game during those days. I would concoct a mixture of technical signals and then back tested those signals with a bunch of stocks to see the win loss rate. I once did that for thirty days non-stop, and you know what, the result I got was a flat win loss rate. That of course did not deter me in the slightest, because I believed firmly that the problem was in the concoction of technical signals, not anywhere else. As soon as I was able to achieve the correct mix of technical signals, all would be good. So I believed.

It was a humbling and frustrating few years, and near the end of my tether, when I was almost on the verge of giving up, I chanced upon the concept of price action or price volume action analysis as some may like to call it.

The premise is that all there is to know about the stock or investment instrument has already been captured in the price as well as its movement. In the case of stocks, we also have the secondary indicator of daily volume as a helpful confirmation.

This was like a god sent message to one who was nearing the end of his line. Finally it made some sense to me. I did not have to bother so much with stochastics, moving averages and Bollinger bands any more. (if all these sound like a foreign language to you, just bear in mind that it does not matter) Price and volume would be all that I cared about.

The idea was simplistic and appealing, yet when trying to apply into the real world, it was really tough in the beginning. Price action was besotted with price levels. There were certain price levels which were deemed as support and resistance bands and you were expected to formulate plans to cater for instances when prices plunged through those bands or when prices rebounded away from said bands.

I tottered along this path for another three years, and I have to say honestly, at that point in time, it did not seem to me that I was getting anywhere. If you pictured a drunken sailor in a pub trying to get out and take the bus, that would be quite an accurate depiction of my stock market investing journey at that time.

It wasn't until I studied, really studied and kept copious records of my trade journals where I finally made some headway into respectable profitability.

Eventually, my personal understanding and usage of the fundamental and technical school of thoughts would be fundamentals should be used for targeting and filtration. I depend on the fundamental side of things to tighten my scope and narrow down which are the stocks I should be interested in. The technical analysis would play its part in determining where and when I should be pulling the trigger to enter, as well as exit the stock positions. This was a marriage of the two great houses, and for me it was a profitable system which catered to my preferences.

At this point, I can understand if you are feeling a little deflated, or perhaps a little curious. Deflated because I have without a doubt stated that there is no holy grail, and curious because of what I did to create that breakthrough for myself.

I would like to reiterate the part about having no holy grail. I mean, it is really no business of mine if you choose not to believe that and go on to splurge thousands of dollars of your hard earned cash on systems from folks who want to sell you. I can only point out that if those systems work so well, the folks selling them will definitely not want you to get their hands on them. This is because technical systems suffer from what we call mass usage effect. When a certain critical mass of people start taking action on the same technical signals, the trade is effectively nullified. Also, even if those systems did not suffer from mass usage effects, why would these folks want to sell them to you for less than ten thousand a pop, when they can be easily making that much a day from those systems?

At the end of the day, there is really no free lunch in the world, and if something really sounds too good to be true, then it usually is.

Now for the part on my breakthrough, short of giving you a personal one on one coaching session to guide you through on what works for me from the technical perspective, it will be very tough to pen it down such that it works for you too. However, there are certain pointers which I stuck to during the climb up.

- Reviewing the trade journal and making correlations to the stock movements
- Looking at the larger time frame in the initial stage. Only after you have a proven set of rules and system would you want to delve into the lower time frames.
- You do not need to hurry, there is no one in the world who can force you to trade, so take your time and initiate the trade only on your terms.
- Be sure to have a set of rules for you to follow. Even if it is just a one liner at the start, build the habit of having rules so that you will have boundaries to operate from.

Some Other Useful Things

In this section, I will be talking about some stuff which I think would be pretty helpful to anyone who is keen on making some money out of investing in the stock market.

Momentum trading

This kind of trading and investment strategy relies heavily on, you guessed it, momentum as the name suggests. In other words, how we develop and execute this strategy would be fairly reliant on the current and expected buying or selling interest.

Strategies can be as simple as, if the stock has had a gap up day, I will resolve to enter into that stock the next day at the opening price. This is due to the fact that the trader expects the upward momentum to continue and hence makes such a move. Similar cases can be made when the stock has had a gap down day.

The crux of the matter here is identifying the momentum which preferably can at least last for a few days, a longer period would of course be much welcome. Many times, folks who are just purely doing momentum based trading would have not so great win loss ratios for their trades, but make up for it with their larger winning margins. It is advisable that we do not just rely solely on momentum but instead seek to incorporate it into our trading systems.

For myself, I use momentum for that extra push in order to get in the extra profits. So in situations where I may have hit my target profit for a particular stock, I may just let the position continue to run if I see momentum in the stock counter.

The way to discern sustainable momentum from the ones which may fizzle out quick would be to recognize that most causes of momentum moves come from the news. It is therefore our job to ascertain quickly and astutely which pieces of news has true impact on the bottom line and which are just daily hogwash. It is quite rare to keep having news which has true impact on the company's earnings potential and value, so we always examine each piece of news quickly in relation to our relevant knowledge of the stock. This also means the more familiar you are with the stock and company, the better you would be at filtering out true news from market noise.

Trend Following

This can be called a strategy and at the same time a general principle which most traders would like to follow. Trade the trend, follow the trend, the trend is your friend would count amongst the many sayings that hammer in the fact that when you are trading and investing in the direction of the trend, you make things easier for yourself.

Picture this. If you have a stock which has a price chart that is basically just moving non linearly upwards over a fairly long period of time, it would be safe to assume that if your intent was to long the stock, you would have a higher probability of getting a winning trade.

I have been in such situations before, and I will tell you it is basically a simple thing to just place your orders at the proper technical levels, wait for the price of the stock to come back and retrace to those said technical levels, and then watch your orders get filled. Then as the stock resumes its upward climb after the retracement, you stand by to take profit or to manage your stock positions. Taking profits can also be an agonizing decision, because you want to lock in profits yet at the same time do not want to leave too much money on the table should the stock continue to meteor upward. Sometimes, I handle it by taking profit with a portion of the holdings, and shifting my mental stop losses to break even for my other existing portion. This effectively creates an idea for me where I would look upon the existing stock holdings as being "free", because the profits taken prior have paid for the purchase of these current stocks. Having free stocks does not mean you can treat them any differently, just that there is that extra little space you give yourself to earn a little lesser, or to gain that much more profits. In such cases, usually it will turn out to be a breakeven for this free portion, or I gather approximately two times more profits as compared to if I were to just close off everything in a whole. My decision to execute this move depends wholly on my assessment of the stock and the company as well as the current technical situation. Of course, I will have to admit that the niggling feeling to take a gamble will usually be the initial instigator for me to consider making this move, though the decision on whether to do so will still be based on facts and numbers.

Trading and investing with the trend has definitely its benefits, which is why so many folks are expounding it and making it their mantra even. It is however, sometimes hard to grasp and formulate into a working investment strategy.

One of the main things is that when you are looking at the trend, you have got to be mindful of what time period you are on. There are different time periods, ranging from the minute charts to monthly charts. No one would argue with you if you were to say that the longer the time frame, the more weightage those price charts would have. This is because a candle on the month chart is a representation of the whole month's price action for that particular stock. The month's struggle between the bulls and the bears as well as the sum aggregate of the resources they committed into the fight is all encapsulated in that month chart. A candle on the one minute chart on the other hand, would definitely have considerably much lesser resources poured into it as compared to the month chart, thereby weakening its level of conviction. Similarly, a trend on the minute chart may be upward, but when the day chart or the month chart is telling a downward story, you can safely ignore the minute chart.

When you are first starting out, it is safest to look at higher period charts, like the day, week and month charts for example. The trends presented on these charts would have a lower probability of turning out to be not sustainable as compared to the lower time periods.

Another thing with trading with the trend would be having sensible entry and exit points. Let us assume you have done your analysis and have identified the stock which you want to pull the trigger on to join in its up trend. It is currently at the price of $50 per share. Some folks may just pull the trigger and jump in at $50. Others may do what I usually do and park orders at predetermined price levels which in this case let us assume it to be $30. If the price does retrace, which price usually does because there are hardly any cases of straight line shooting up or down, then I will get into the stock at a better price. This also means I have lesser to lose than a person who went in at $50 simply because my price is closer to the "ground" so to speak. Generally speaking, when your stock entry price is closer to the ground, where ground means $0, then you have got a more stable position, very much like a lower centre of gravity in the laws of physics.

A person who buys at $50 versus a person who buys at $30 would have different feelings purely because of the different entry prices. The $30 guy would have more space for the stock to move. Think about it, if the price of the stock moves to $40, that presents a $10 gain for the $30 guy but a $10 loss to the $50 person. This business with having a sensible entry and exit point would of course have to be grounded with a fair dose of technical analysis. Entry and exit points have to be mapped and determined from the technical levels and then the next thing to do is to have the mentality of being able to give up the trade.

What? Did I hear it correctly?

Yes you did. Have the mental preparation of giving up the trade. Why is that so? This is for the times when the retracement happens, but it does not hit your technically determined level. So instead of dropping to $30, it drops to $33, and then stages a rebound. This is also for the times when there is no retracement, and the price continues to rumble upwards from $50.

You do get such situations. That is why you have got to always have the mental preparation to let go of the trade and move on to the next one. This is also the reason why your investment and trading system can never be too restrictive such that you only have one or two triggers a year. Imagine if you missed your last trade trigger, you might have to wait till the next year in order to have another chance.

I would also like to point out that in our example, the $50 guy may not necessarily be wrong, but it is just my style to err on the side of caution. If the $50 guy has got the gumption and necessary resources to stomach the potential bumpier ride than the $30 guy, I would say kudos to him. The $50 guy would be what I call a "jumper". These guys usually jump into a trade for fear of missing out. In times when the momentum is raging and the news is on point and really has deep fundamental impact, jumpers rule the roost. There is simply no space for folks who prefer entry on retracements because there simply are none.

In those kinds of situation, you either jump or you move on to the next potential stock. Mentality and psychology plays a large part on whether you would be a suitable jumper. And we all know that trading psychology is affected largely by the amount of cash that is at risk at any one point in time. If you want to train yourself to be a jumper, yet find yourself lacking the necessary mental requirements, the answer would be to start small. Risk small amounts when jumping until you get used to the feel of it. Then you would be able to gradually scale up to a manageable amount.

I myself am not much of a jumper, but I do jump when the occasion presents itself. Jumping is like any other skill in the trading and investment world, always good to add into your arsenal so that you may call upon it whenever you think you need it.

How do you determine trend would be another headache for some folks, where some would subscribe to the idea of using moving averages to determine the trend while others would deem that the usage of Bollinger bands be the one true way of determining trend.

I have come to realize, after probably thousands of hours looking at charts, is that when the trend is evident, it is so obvious that you do not need any indicators or new-fangled technology to help you say that it is a trend. Visual inspection of the chart is all you need. For me, I would like to be on the higher time frame and then do a visual scanning to determine what looks like the immediate trend that is gripping the market at the moment. Moving from top left to bottom right would mean it is a downward trend. Going from bottom left to top right would mean the bulls are in control. When you look and look, and cannot see anything obvious, then that is what we mean by a trendless situation or a sideways market. When a market goes sideways, it usually means there is a battle between the bulls and the bears and the results are not known as yet.

Sideways markets are great situations for day trading by the way, because you have what you deem as a fairly rectangular shape kind of chart. This means there is a fairly defined top and bottom boundary for you to day trade in. We will not delve too deep into this day trading aspect right now, probably more in a future book perhaps.

So no need to over complicate things, visual inspection usually works best because it is the most simple, and when things are simple, they usually are in their truest form.

The Need For Stop Losses

This concept has been expounded in this book at various junctures but I thought it is worth a section on its own, just because of its importance in the world of trading and investment.

A stop loss or cut loss is basically a predetermined price point which is the exit signal for anyone to get out of a trade that has gone bad. The concept of having an amount which is comfortable for that particular person to lose will come into play here.

Say Adam has determined that he is ready to risk $1000 on a certain trade call, and he has a hundred shares which are currently trading at the price point of $40. This would then mean that his stop loss price point if the trade call were a long would be at $30, because his $1000 risked money will be divided by his hundred shares to yield a price space of $10. His trade would then have the space to gyrate up to $30, and if the price point were to fall below it, then he would close off the trade, dust himself off, and then look on to the next one.

This point is also the part where I would like to emphasize the importance of the candle or bar close on which ever time frame you are monitoring. If you are a day trader, you might be looking at the hourly candle close. This means if the price of the stock ever trades below $30 on any hourly candle close, you would execute the close of the trade. However, if you were a swing or longer term investor, you could be looking at the day candle close or even the week candle close. This would mean that you would only execute the exit strategy when the stock trades and closes below $30 on the day or week candle, depending on the time frame that you are observing. Bear in mind that the longer the time frame, the more conviction it will possess because of the sheer amount of resources used to build and compete for that particular candle's result.

This point will also lead to another contentious area that has been open to debate for quite a long while. Some folks will argue that if one were to follow this style, the total amount incurred in losses would be higher than the comfortable amount you are willing to lose. This is because while we are waiting for the day or week candle to close, the price may drop even further after crashing through the predetermined mark. Taking the previous example into account, you might encounter prices at $25 or even $20 when your price level was supposed to be $30. This would result in having to lose double the amount you were willing to fork out.

For me, I acknowledge the flaws of this way utilizing the stop loss, but I choose to still have it this way because of the advantages it confers. The one major advantage you have when you execute the stop loss upon a close would be that you would be spared situations where the price spikes up or down drastically and then does not close at all.

Take again our example of Adam and his stock. His designated stop loss price was $30. If his stock moves down heavily within the hour, say to $20, and yet he still manages to hold his nerve and tell himself to wait for the hour close, he might find that on the hour close, the stock price has rebounded back to $35 perhaps. This then creates what we term as a pin bar or a hammer as what the candle stick enthusiasts would call.

What Adam has achieve by holding his nerve would be getting out of a situation which would have flushed his stop loss. He is still in the game despite the intra hourly downward move which proved to be nothing but just a scare.

These situations can happen on all time frames, so bear in mind that the larger the time frame, the more resources that have to be committed.

What to do then with the issue of potentially having to see almost double of what you were initially willing to lose? The answer is to trade in smaller amounts. Imagine this time for Adam, instead of a hundred shares, he has only an exposure of fifty shares because he knows the weakness of using the stop loss on close, he has easily circumvented the issue and still maintained his comfortable amount to lose.

So when I say this, usually I get met with some hoots and derision, because some folks will then say, won't the profit potential be similarly reduced? The answer of course is a yes, and I would like to remind everyone now that it is always first about what you can and are willing to lose, before we go on to talk about profit and gains. If we are able to secure a firm foundation on our losses, then profits will naturally follow. This is due to the fact that your trading psychology will be more stable and less subject to the whims and sways of the market wind.

Of course, not everyone subscribes to this theory. Some swear by the touch and go stop loss, where it literally means if the price ever touches

$30 like in our earlier example, then the trade would be stopped out. There is no talk about waiting for a close on whatever time period.

The trader in this case would have a tighter management of his loss amount, because any time $30 is hit, his trade will be out. However, that also means his chances of being flushed out of his stop will also be much higher than a trader who was using the close stop loss method.

For me, it is no right or wrong way of doing things. It again boils back down to persona and trading psychology. For the folks who enjoy loads of action, I see them being more inclined to using the touch stop way of handling stop losses, whilst the folks who are a little more relaxed and easy, they tend to wait for more confirmation, and hence employ the close stop loss method.

I used to subscribe to the touch stop, because that was the more popular and more widely taught. However, I did not like the feeling of always being on the right side of the trade only to miss it because of being flushed out of the position. It is like a double slap to the face. You make a loss, and you end up being right in the trade call. That is the reason why the close stop came into play for me and so far it has been working well in my opinion.

Of course, these two ways of handling stop losses are way superior to one other way of handling stop loss, which is having no stop loss. Honestly I cannot say this enough, but here is my reiteration again, always have a stop loss, even if it is just a mental price level. Keep that level in mind and when it is breached, you will have to execute the exit. It is a campaign, where every trade is a battle. If a stop loss is breached, you know you have lost the battle, but the war is still ongoing as long as you have resources. Always have a stop loss.

One more point to note would be this. The determination of the price level for a stop loss has to make sense from the market analysis perspective. What do I mean by that? In the Adam example, the $30 price point was determined purely by the amount Adam was willing to lose and his share exposure. This is not the way, and the example was held up only to illustrate how the stop loss should operate.

In every trade call, you should always have two things in mind first. The entry price, or the price you are willing to pay to partake in fortunes of the stock, and also the stop loss price which is determined by your market analysis methods. In many cases, people will turn to technical analysis in order to get a stop loss price. They will derive price levels from their support and resistance lines and have those price points ear marked as plausible stop losses. This then is also the reason why the role of technical analysis is often remarked by me to be more of a precision instrument, whilst that of fundamental analysis would be more of a filtration system to get your good, worthwhile stocks.

This also means, when choosing your stop loss levels, you should not have too tight a stop. For instance in the Adam example, if his entry price was $40, and there happened to be a minor support level at $38, and Adam was actually planning his trade for the longer haul, it would be quite tough to place his stop at $38. As a rule of thumb, a longer trading period would usually require a larger stop loss. Similarly, when you play longer and have a larger stop loss, usually your profit targets will also be larger. This is to maintain a proper risk reward ratio for each trade.

One thing that I was guilty of in the past was to pick and choose tighter stop losses, because that enabled me to have larger share exposure and hence make more profits, at least in my mind that is! I would choose a tight stop and then honestly hope that the market does not touch that level. Some of my trades were so ridiculously structured that I may be in a trade and then out of the trade within a couple of minutes, with a couple of hundred losses to boot. This was especially so when I was still doing the touch stop loss. It is no point looking good on paper and hoping that the market does not touch the stop loss. It is also no good to start counting the profits even before starting the trade.

Engaging in such mental gymnastics would only drain your energy and leave you wanting when you actually need it.

That is the reason why almost all trades that end up as wins will start with the first question of how much we can lose. There are just facts and figures on hand, and lesser hope and wishful thinking. It is important for us to see things as what they are, not what we wish them to be.

Some Other Stuff You May Want To Know

Stock screeners.

These things are so common these days, with most of them being online and accessed via web browsers. The primary use of stock screeners would be to provide some form of automated help when we are dealing with the tedious task of filtering companies to look out for.

In this universe of hundreds of thousands of stocks, screeners can help much with just some clicks of the mouse and we will have a more manageable short list of a few hundreds. Okay, that was almost a half joke, but to be honest, sometimes you really got to crawl through a few hundred companies in order to get to those which are worthy of being traded.

Insiders and institutional investors

These guys are considered the folks who know more about their companies as well as being the heavy hitters. Knowing their tracks would give us retail investors a major leg up when it comes to our investing decisions.

Looking at specific websites reporting such movements and even browsing the annual reports to get a sense of who's who and who's doing what might be good, but it could present too much of a cognitive burden. Imagine you are monitoring your short list of fifty different stocks, and you have got to keep track of the insider and institutional trades. That drove me up the wall.

A simpler way which I found for myself would be to utilize and trust the idea of the technical analysts. That which needs to be known has all been captured by the stock price. I embrace this idea when it comes to dealing with monitoring of stocks which have been already shortlisted. However, when it comes to putting together the shortlist, there literally is no running away from the heavy legwork that comes with the fundamental analysis.

For me, fundamental analysis with its usual grunt work will lead the way for my creation of my monitoring shortlist of stocks, then technical analysis will give me the pricing levels to execute my investment ideas.

CHAPTER 4

Rule Number Four (Facts And Numbers To Help You)

This area is where we are delving deeper into the fun world of stock market fundamental analysis. This would consist of looking at company numbers and figuring them out to see if they make the cut for us to monitor them. The big question is always how do we do that?

The Value Question

This is always one of the first things you will encounter when you come up to anyone who is looking at the stock market through the lenses of a fundamentalist. Does this company represent value and is the value already realized by the stock market?

Some folks live and breathe the idea that you can solely rely on fundamentals to invest in the stock market. They are not wrong. I have seen and been in touch with people who have never seen a stock chart in their lives, and yet they have gone on to make millions investing in the stock market. One of the more common denominators to these people are the following:

- They start out with more than normal quantities of resources as compared to the average joe on the street.
- As a result they tend to have a better grip on their trading psychology on the average
- They tend to make their money on occasions when the markets have drastic movements, which means they are definitely not day traders or short term investors.
- Occasions that come to mind are like the 2000 tech bubble burst, as well as the 2008 mortgage notes crisis or the Lehman crisis.
- They do not need to depend on the earnings from their investments for their day to day living and expenses.

Fundamentals could be all you need to get ahead in the game of investing in the stock market. You use fundamentals to pick a good stock, and then steadfastly wait for either the stock price to be depressed such that it becomes a no brainer for you to buy the stock, then sell it when the overall market becomes overly buoyant, to cash in on the greed of others.

This would mean loads of patience, because you would then need to wait for that afore said event, which would bring the stock price below the value that you know it has. Usually the no brainers would be systemic events, where the overall stock market is affected and all counters take the hit. This is because when the fear is so widespread, it affects all counters without really accounting for much logic or thought. This also means that the prices getting depressed have a higher probability of just being affected by sentiment rather than having any real structural issues within the company. If the event were just centred on the specific company, then more brain work would be needed to sieve through the facts and noise in order to determine if the value which you previously saw in the company still exists.

Investing via fundamentals is really a game of waiting, where you wait to get in, and then you wait further to get out. To be honest, it is not cut out for all folks. I mean, if we look at a simple situation of a normal middle class family, where both adults are out to work and you know they have some excess cash every month which they place in the bank account. For these folks who may have built up a small nest egg of say $50000, to get them to plunk it all down during a period of depression, when stock prices are mostly low, would be easy to say on paper, but harder to do without any form of practice.

These folks probably would be better off having constant exposure and learning as well as understanding more about their investing and trading psyche, which will then place them in a much better stead during big opportunities presented in times of financial turmoil.

Think too about the person who wishes to day trade, because he may have a sizeable sum to start off with, but because of his decision to rely on that sum to generate his monthly income, this method of fundamental investing may not be quick enough to sustain a reasonable lifestyle.

So my view stands that fundamental investing is all good and is perfectly able to stand on its own two feet. It is just like bringing a sword to a battlefield. It is a worthy weapon to have. And now I pose this question to you. Why bring one sword, when you can actually wield two?

My personal take on this is as what I have mentioned earlier in the other segments. I use fundamental analysis for the purposes of filtration because that is the innate strength of looking at fundamentals. You get to see, as far as numbers and annual reports are concerned, the strength and competencies of a company. This ensures that I will only restrict my trading and investing shortlist to companies which have good and proper standing. I mean, if we are interested in

Starbucks, we probably can summarize their business as selling coffee, and that is how we would shape our thinking and look at other facets of their business model.

Having the sword of fundamental analysis with you gives you the ability to pick and choose amongst the huge pool of stock candidates out there, and that would increase your chances of winning. And yes, I shall drop the references to weapons right here and now in case it may offend certain folk.

The other instrument which I would wield alongside reading the fundamentals, would of course be that of using technical analysis, or chart reading, as some would call it. If fundamentals are able to provide the boundary for which you are able to herd and choose your companies, then technical analysis would give you the timing and signals to pull them out of the water and engage with them.

One gives you the system of filtration, the other gives you the system of engagement.

Let's have a look at what we usually look for in a company in order to determine if it has the potential to represent value.

Increasing Profits

Profits represent growth, and growth usually gives value and that translates to a winning investment for people like us investing in the stock market. What is better than profits? Well, increasing profits year on year. That would be great news actually to any vested person whose company is seeing such growth.

Usually, profit numbers can be easily gotten from the company's annual reports under the income statement portion. Most reports these days give at least a one year comparison to the most recent set of reported figures, but that would not be sufficient. For the folks who deign not to use the power of the internet, they would then need to collate and flip through all the physical annual reports of the company for preferably ten years. If you can obtain fifteen, it would be even better. Remember, when we have more data, our brain acts like those of the artificial intelligence with their deep learning algorithms, we absorb and are able to process more.

I used to love to do that, because I just like to flip through reports. Something about the paper and the smell of it just drew me to it. I have to admit though, it was painstaking work. Honestly. After you went through three companies, you would probably start seeing stars. That is the reason why I would encourage all to utilize the technology that is available to us all. These days, you can easily take a look at the ten year performance of a firm and zero in on its profit metric.

A good indicator would be a situation where you see year on year gradual, growth. This usually tells you that the company has got steady sales and at the same time, is also expanding to fill up the market potential. We would keep an eye out for the gross profit, while paying more attention to the net profit number. We want to see what the cost of sales and goods are to the company too. This way you would be able to figure out the company's margin and that can be a useful thing to have in your head.

When I see gradual growth which is then punctuated by a sudden growth spurt, I have my sensors put out. To be honest, I don't really fancy such situations and would most definitely have to take a closer look at it. This is the time when you got to really go into the annual reports first, probably using at least three annual reports. I always take the preceding annual report, annual report for the growth spurt year, and the annual report after. You would want to investigate what was the cause of the growth spurt and the key question would be if it were sustainable. Many companies have such spurts on paper, and it shows up incredibly well, only to have it known later that profits were actually due to a one off sale of some asset. It is our duty to find out what is happening, and make careful, factual judgements for ourselves, because it will build up our conviction when we go on to the decision making phase.

Increasing Sales

The revenue or sales numbers are sometimes able to predict the profits because some industries record their sales numbers but do not book the profits until after the projects or goods are delivered. Sales numbers would be a good benchmark to assess any company and of course, we would want increasing sales year on year as evidence of having a growth company in our sights.

For some companies, their sales and profit numbers may register little or no growth, perhaps one or two percent per year. Counters like Macdonald's and General Electric would come into mind. These are more stable, steady counters that have engaged their market potential and are likely to just cruise along. What they represent to the investor would be cash in the forms of dividends as well as value creation via company stock buy backs. If well run, these behemoths usually would be sitting on stockpiles of cash, which are usually distributed as dividends to the shareholders or used in corporate stock purchases. Corporate stock purchases tend to boost the stock price per share because the purchases reduce the total number of shares available in the market.

Some would then ask, what would be the point of looking at such slow growing companies? Remember, our task is to pick and filtrate those companies which are well managed and are fitting to our criteria for being listed in our target pool. Though these bigger firms may not have the sales and profit growth figures, they do represent value when they have depressions in their stock prices due to either external or internal shocks. This is the reason why it would also be a good idea to have a handle of what would be a fair price for these stocks such that you would know if its under or overvalued.

Granted, if we were able to choose, it would be great to go for growth companies any day of the year, especially when we are en route to building more financial resources. For those who have a better piece of the pie or perhaps a piece of silver or gold in the spoons that were used to feed you, then the larger firms with bigger and more consistent dividend pay outs may make some sense for some resources to be parked there.

For me, when it comes to assessing sales and profit numbers, you can find year after year of constant growth. It is possible, though not super common. What do you do then with figures that have their ups and downs? A quick rule of thumb is assessing how many down years are present in that ten year period. If it is anything more than three, I wouldn't really look too much deeper in, unless all those three years were bunched together closer to the front, and the more recent numbers are all showing constant growth.

The key takeaway I want to impress upon everyone here is that we are trying to build a story with these numbers and facts. No airy fairy castles in the air kind of stuff but good old solid facts and figures. A company with some dips and some growth punctuated in a random fashion over a ten or fifteen year period would convey a message to me that either there is something wrong with the management of the company, or it is in a cyclical industry. If we are still interested in the company after knowing all these, then we can have the wherewithal to investigate further.

When it comes to me though, I like to go on the least path of resistance. What this means is I would rather trade or invest in a company that has constant growth as shown on their ten year period report, rather than into a company with splotchy growth numbers. Some may argue this. Yes indeed I may lose out on the unpolished gem and yes sometimes these splotchy growth numbers actually indicate something better. However, I always think that with the universe of stocks standing as it is, there will always be hefty chance for me to rope in the profits just as well riding on the growth firms. You can call me lazy, but it is just me. I prefer to sink more effort in searching for the no brainer growth stocks than to expend effort on investigating if a splotchy one is worth the bite.

Low Liabilities

We have looked at sales and profit numbers, so now we will look at the liabilities and debts of the company we may become interested in. For this segment, it is important to take note of two major things. The long term debt or liabilities, as well as the current debt.

For the current debt, which is usually characterized by any liabilities that are callable by the creditors within a year, we would want to see the company's cash reserves being able to pay off the total current debt. The higher the ratio of cash to current debt is, the better we would rate the company.

For the long term debt, we usually utilize this metric debt to equity ratio to see the potential state of health for the firm we are interested in. Equity is the value of the firm that belongs to the shareholders, which are folks like you and me. So in this case, we want the ratio to be as low as possible, because that would mean that the debt which has got to be paid off to creditors is much lesser than the value attributable to us shareholders.

Having lesser debt in the company is also a good situation because it indicates that the company may not need to tap on debt as yet to fuel its growth. This typically happens when the company is in a fast growing industry that has loads of demand, or when the company has significant barriers to entry via their product or services and they are able to command premium prices.

Eventually though, all companies tend to reach a stage where they would find it cheaper to take on debt in order to fuel their expansion plans. The trick here is we do not want to see a potential target firm get sucked into a debt trap where they take on too much debt for their own good. A debt to equity ratio of approximately 0.5 or lesser would be a good gauge of what we are aiming for.

We most definitely do not want to see a situation where the company is actually using debt to fund its operating expenses. This is normally a bad signal, because it purely states that the operating costs cannot be met by normal operating profits or cashflow alone. However, this does not mean that the company is beyond redemption, as I have seen firms which managed to do turnarounds despite being saddled with debts. It is also foolhardy to think of shorting or short selling these companies, as I have heard so many people wonder. If I cannot buy these companies, why don't I short sell them instead? These debt saddled firms are not all in danger of collapsing under their own weight. They may yet be able to sustain this façade of respectable operations for years or even decades, hence it would be foolhardy to short these companies just on the basis of this one debt metric.

Increasing Return On Equity

The return on equity is effectively the net profits of the firm divided by the total value attributed to the shareholders. This figure represents how hard the money in the shareholder pot would have worked over the past year. Higher net profits would mean a better return, which then indicates that the shareholders would tend to have a better time. I mean, more bang for the individual buck right?

Why this metric is important is also due to the possibility of stock issuance by the company. When stock issuance happens, the total number of shares in the market are increased, which also means the total equity value of the firm would also increase. If the company's profits were to grow on a steady rate, but yet be met by such an increase in equity, it would be somewhat negative news because the profit would be so called shared amongst more hands.

An increasing return on equity percentage would be a most welcome sight then, because it essentially means that the company is making better use of its equity to generate more returns for its stockholders.

Now, some folks might ask, then would this same issue of having profits shared by more folks happen during a stock split? The quick answer is no, and here is why. A stock split is essentially a situation where a $100 per share stock is split into typically two parts, thereby creating a situation where it becomes $50 a share after the split. There is no infusion of additional shareholder value to broaden the equity base.

Barriers To Entry

Another factor to think about when assessing the viability of a stock would be the qualitative aspect of its barriers to entry. How tough is it for would be competitors to enter the same space and have a free for all with that company?

Take Starbucks for instance, what it is selling is beyond a cup of premium priced coffee, it is actually selling the Starbucks experience which happens the moment any of its customers step into the store. I mean, coffee is easily made right? You could do it yourself, but why would you want to specifically pop down to a Starbucks store and have them make that similar coffee and then charge you a premium for it? That in itself is one of the barriers to entry which Starbucks has successfully planted as a strong defence against would be competitors.

Sometimes, barriers to entry may not be company induced. They could very well be results of government policies. Let's go a little afield here for this example. In the south east Asian country of Singapore, they have a federal rule that mandates all vehicles that are three years or older to go for an annual vehicular check by an authorized agent. Guess what? There are only a couple of such authorized agents around in the country, and that effectively makes it an oligopoly. To add on to the attractiveness of this industry, it is a well-known fact that getting the government to authorize another new agent is almost a nigh impossible task.

If you were an investor staring at this kind of scenario, just focusing on the barriers to entry factor would give you fairly positive vibes on this. An industry with just two players, and you have got a government rule which literally ensures the demand for the services provided. Some may be tempted to draw parallels to Boeing and Airbus, but the industry which these two behemoths are in are actually quite different in nature. Airplane purchases tend to be cyclical in nature, with airlines tending to place their fleet orders in a guesstimate of how their future demand would be like. As such, aircraft manufacturers then are subject to this cyclical demand wave that ebbs and flows. For the car inspection industry, the demand there is a virtual constant. You do not have to worry about when your next customers will appear.

Another kind of barrier would be the high switching costs entailed should the customer wish to switch from one brand to the next. This is real, just think of your pc to mac switch. I mean if you are a successful dual system user, then kudos to you. For those who have been born and bred on the pc, switching to the mac is pretty much like giving birth, tough and painful. For those who have been weaned on the mac, getting on to the pc would perhaps seem like a downgrade.

We want to get companies with as many barriers to entry as possible, or to get companies with a couple of very strong barriers. This ensures the niche in which the prospective target companies are in would not be crowded out too quickly due to new entrants. One thing to note however, it is my opinion that no barrier will last forever. Things always come up, government legislation changes, technology disrupts. Any of those factors can be a cause of change and create a ripple effect which breaks down the erstwhile solid fortress of a barrier.

So the trick here is to get into companies which have existing good barriers, and then observe how the management is making pathways into creating new barriers in preparation for the day when their old barriers become obsolete. This is something which I would term as a good to have, but not particularly needful in the initial stages of stock filtration.

Why?

There would simply be information overload when you have to consider so many moving factors and levers. Attempting to see what the management of one company is doing might be possible, but when you have got to do it repetitively for five or six hundred, it might seem totally arduous. When that comes into play, the danger of being complacent would become real. You have sooo many companies to look through within an allocated span of time that your brain would be tempted to short-cut the process. In doing so, the usual robustness and careful examination as well as thought analysis would be compromised.

This is the reason why I would encourage folks to just focus on seeking out the barriers to entry first, without considering if the management are drawing up any plans for future barriers.

Another thing to note would be to be clear headed. You definitely do not want to start imagining barriers to entry just because you are so besotted with any particular company. Generally speaking, the shorter the explanation of the barrier of entry, the clearer and stronger it should be. You can try explaining it to anyone. It would be even better if the person has absolutely zero knowledge of the company or stocks. If they also get what you are trying to say in the shortest possible time, you might have a winner here in terms of the strength and simplicity of the barrier to entry.

Management

Closely related to barriers to entry would be the management team of the company in question. When this factor is judged to be strong, it can also be listed as one of the barriers to entry.

Just like the captain that steers the ship on the ocean, the management or decision maker of the company would similarly be responsible for moving the firm through the choppy waters of business. A strong and capable captain would ensure the ship's survival and prosperity, as would a strong management.

The key issue here is learning how to correctly identify good and strong management. I mean, we are retail investors for the most part, not hedge fund managers like Peter Lynch who can fly all over the country and pop into the company headquarters for a look. The lucky thing here is, in this day and age of social media, there aren't many things which can't be ferreted out if you are of mind.

We take a look at their track record.

Simply key in their names into Google and you should be able to at least have a sniff whether they have had any management experiences of any kind. Take a look at the current state of their previous companies and also bear in mind when was their date of leaving, then track back four or five years' worth of annual reports prior to their move.

Another thing is looking at their personal preferences in terms of where they stay and what they drive. Personally, I am more of a fan for those folks who are a little more down to earth and a little less flashy. That is not to say I haven't had home runs with companies run by flashy loud people, it is just my personal preference.

In general, I tend to find that those who are a little less loud would probably let their actions do the talking. They don't need flash cars and big mansions, but prefer to let their results speak for themselves. We won't have to look far to have the legendary Warren Buffett as an example. Okay, you might say he is a mite extreme, and the world just don't make them like that anymore. Well, there are countless of other folks who are icons for the less flashy lifestyle and I am sure you will be able to identify them.

Another thing I want to point out would be the kid with the midas touch. There always just seem to be someone like that. A person who magically turns around an ailing company, sets up new companies and they instantly become a hit. When the company has such a charismatic leader, I would tend to focus more on the numbers and hard facts. The reason being I am worried that the valuation of the company would somehow factor in the "brightness" of the star leader, and once that shine is no longer there, the company might take a hit. Also, when we encounter such a charismatic leader, there might be all round positive reports which may lead us to being easily carried away in the feel good moment. This is something which I am always wary of, hence I will tend to use numbers and facts to ground myself. If there aren't sufficient numbers, then I will choose to skip the company and hunt for the next better one.

Valuation

This may be the multi-billion dollar question when it comes to fundamental analysis. All fundies would want to have a number which they can use to compare with the current trading price. This is how people will come up with terms like under or over valuation. The benchmark which the trading price is compared to would be the valuation number that is derived.

So how do we actually derive the valuation number then? Turns out if you were to run a simple google search, you will be able to turn up at least three or more different kinds of valuation methods that are purported to be used by Wall Street experts. Let's talk about them a little here, about the methods, not the Wall Street experts.

First up would be the grand-daddy of them all, the discounted cash flow analysis. As the name suggests, it is a method which involves many numbers, and if you were to manually punch in the numbers on a calculator, it may take you a little while to get to your final destination. Trust me, I have done it before. Thankfully, we have excel spread sheets and a plethora of other technological wonders that can automate this process for us so the key numbers that we are concerned with would be very much reduced.

We would want to know the current operating cash flow of the company. This can be easily gotten from the latest annual reports, so no issues here. The next number in question would the assumed growth rate which you would want to tag on to the said company.

Normally, how we would calculate this would be to have around ten years' worth of data in terms of revenue and profit. We then check the growth rates year on year and take an average of the nine periods. Once we have both revenue and profit average growth rates, the prudent course of things would be to utilize the lower of the two rates. I mean, being prudent is always better in most cases. Some folks however, tend to be a bit more of a purist when it comes to such things, so they take another average of the two averages. Nonetheless, whichever the case may be, the end result would be to retrieve a projected company growth rate which can be reasonably relied upon.

I say reasonably because there is no one on earth who can give a definite prediction of what the true growth rate of the company will be. Too many factors on hand which may complicate the count and we shall have to make do with the best approximation that we can reach.

After the growth rate of the company, we will then have to come up with the proper discount rate, which usually is the cost of capital needed to fund and operate the company. There is a fancy acronym for this, called WACC. It simply means weighted average cost of capital. In a company, there are both equity and debt. The cost of debt would be the interest rate which the debt market charges the company. Think in terms of the bank, who allows you to borrow funds to buy that house or car. You have got to pay interest on those loans. The same goes for the company and that average interest would be the cost of debt. The cost of equity would be simply the average return on equity. WACC is then calculated by taking exact proportions of debt as well as equity over the total asset value of the company and multiplying with its relevant costs.

Though it isn't super important to what we are doing, the purist in me just had to put it out for the record.

So WACC would be calculated as such

Equity Value Divided By Total Asset Value Multiplied by Cost Of Equity

+

Debt Value Divided By Total Asset Value Multiplied by Cost of Debt Multiplied by One Minus the prevailing tax rate

There you have it. Knock yourself out with WACC.

So in discounted cash flow analysis, when we have these three important numbers, it would be kind of easy to generate that ultimate golden number, which actually is the final sum of all operating cash flows projected forwards into the future using the presumed growth rate, then discounted back into the present using the WACC.

Another way of arriving at the valuation number, would be via the Price Earnings Ratio or multiple. PE ratio for short, it is taken to be the result of getting the current price divided by earnings per share of the stock.

Some folks would once again utilize about ten years' worth of data in order to find out the average PE ratio, then multiply it to the current earnings per share in order to get a grasp of what the likely value of the company should be.

If you aren't already swimming in a lot of ifs, buts and assumptions, it would be high time to recognize that you would be doing that a lot whilst doing DCF and even PE valuation. At the end of the day, no matter how sophisticated the financial model may be, the underlying fact is that it will always be built upon assumptions. Assumptions that may be changeable or unpredictable due to the simple fact that we are trying to project too far into the future.

Let's face it, folks in the seventies would probably have had a good guess of what eighties life style would be. Folks now would probably have a harder time guessing how the future ten years would turn out to be. With the advent of self-driving cars, artificial intelligence and deep learning, technology is both the creator and the destroyer. Who's to say it cannot destroy or restore the hopes and dreams of a company?

I know, it may sound like a super wet blanket to be talking like this at the moment. I mean, you can probably go, then what's the use of doing all these fundie analysis? It's all going down the drain since we cannot predict the future.

Fear not.

DCF or PE or other kinds of financial models that churn out valuation numbers will still be a tentative guide for us. It is by no mean the be all and end all of the decision making process. When we have a DCF valuation number, we have a very rough idea if this company is currently over or under valued. Our main basis is to still to filtrate and form a pool of prospective target companies using all the above fundamental analysis aspects. Looking at growth from the revenue and profit perspective, bringing in qualitative aspects as well as rounding it up with the valuation numbers, these would be tuned toward company selection. We will not base buy or sell decisions just solely off valuation numbers.

Buy and sell decisions will come chiefly from the work from the next section.

CHAPTER 5

Rule Number Five (Master The Mystic Arts)

In this segment, we will concern ourselves with the issue of timing. I mean, from the earlier portion about identification of potential home run stocks, we will have to choose a time on when we need to take a stand with those chosen stocks. Figuring out the intrinsic value will not do us any good if we do not simply get our skin in the game.

This portion is all about letting us know when should be the windows of optimal timing with which to place our stake and watch the drama unfold. I am not talking about placing your trades during the times when the moonlight shines the brightest or during the winter solstice or summer equinox. That is not what I mean when we are talking about windows of optimal timing. There are schools of thought which believe in such trading methodology but I have yet to meet a truly consistently successful performer who employs such arts.

The window of opportunity that will present itself to us actually boils down to the movement of price. The price of the chosen stock, which we have sieved through countless hundreds via our fundamental analysis.

Why is this guy talking about price, what does he actually mean? Those could be the questions running through your head right now and you are absolutely right to have them. The answers all lie with technical analysis of the stock market.

Technical Analysis And How To Train For It

Before you go all excited and eager to learn and unleash this supposed holy grail instrument of mass destruction for the stock market, think again. I have always said there is no such thing as a holy grail. Ditto for technical analysis.

To recap again, technical analysis is the study of the movements and fluctuations of the price as well as volume numbers of the chosen stock or counter. This is because it is believed that the price is the honest ultimate reflection of what the market thinks about the stock. It is the culmination of all the insider trading, the institutional investing, the retail and large scale trading that finally aggregates itself into a single price for that particular time period. As the price moves, technical analysts track how it moves and then make forecasts or decisions based on those movements.

As I have said before, the schools of technical analysis are far and wide, with many utilizing technical signalling devices in order to make their call. I personally do not practise those ways because I have tried them before and found that this kind delayed signalling does not really work for me.

Think about it, a moving average is in essence the average of the prices over a stated period of time, the longer the period of average, the smoother and less reactive it would be to the actual price. This is a common theme running through most of the technical indicators we have today in all markets. They are all derivatives of price and hence would then tend to be somewhat laggy as compared to actual price movement. Consequently, their powers of prediction are also somewhat off.

For me, I personally like to work with the actual price itself. It is cleaner, and actually a whole lot simpler to process. You do not have to concern yourself with all the different parameters of the technical indicator, nor do you have to worry about changing those said parameters in order to suit a particular trading period or style.

Many folks however, treat price action as some sort of mystic art. I, too had those thoughts when I was enamoured with finding the perfect parameter for my stochastics and Relative Strength Index indicator. I have come to realize, the reason why technical indicators are still popular and widely used today is because it is somewhat like the elementary school. It is easy to grasp, and definitely easy to use. Anyone with just a little familiarization practice could just set it up and start investing immediately based off the signals. There is also the hype as well of course, where many folks have come out in the open and touted the superiority of their technical systems. Some claims would entail working only for one hour a day and getting passive income to replace your day job. Others would go for the big ticket and claim millionaire status within six or even three months.

Sadly, there will always be folks who fall for these claims.

It represents money without having to put in too much effort, while it also retains the believability because you are actually still involved. You are the one to set the system up, wait for the signal and then decide on triggering the trade based on the signal. Many people, like me at first, would baulk at learning price action technical analysis because it just seems so wide and vast, and there was no structure or system to babysit us.

I would like to tell you this to be not exactly true. There is a structure of sorts, and you definitely will be able to learn price action if you honestly put in the effort. Let's talk about what kind of efforts you would need to put in.

Candlesticks

Japanese candlesticks may seem daunting, with their many myriad combinations. Patterns that involve a single candlestick, three, five and even seven sticks! All these could sound potentially mind boggling but there is some good news on the horizon.

You may go ahead and master all the Japanese candlestick patterns, it will be your express choice and it is purely an option. You do not need to master all patterns. I will repeat this. You do not need to master all patterns.

For me, I am more concerned with single candlestick signals and what they tend to present in terms of bull or bear indications.

Two of the most commonly searched for candlesticks in my book would be the toppish or bearish shooting star.

It looks like an inverted t. It is usual that the body of the candle is shorter than that of the wick or the shadow or tail. Multiple names but all mean the part that is pointing upward. The reason why there is a long tail is that there was an upward movement during the time period. Take the example of a day shooting star candle. During the day, there was bullish intent and the price was pushed up, however, whether it was just a fake flush by the stop hunters or a real push by the bulls which ended up failing, the bears took over and pushed the price back down. This creates the longish tail.

With a shooting star, this represents bearish intent for the coming periods and we will thus prepare ourselves for it. The usual way of how we search for such candlesticks would be near resistance price levels and bands. If there were to be quite a number clustered together, it would tell a story that the bulls attempted to push through that price level but failed and hence ceding control over to the bears. When spotted, our natural intent would be to short that particular counter.

The other common candlestick pattern would be of the bullish intent, which is commonly known as the hammer. Why? It literally looks like one when presented in the candlestick format. It is quite the opposite of the shooting star, with the long tail pointing downward instead of upwards.

As you might have guessed, bears tried to push the price down, failed in that attempt during that specific period, and the bulls charged the price back up again. This is usually a bullish candle.

At this point in time, I would like to take the chance to state quite categorically that you do not have to be too anal with analyzing candlestick patterns. What I mean is, as long as the candle approximates to a shooting star or a hammer, then acknowledge it as such. There is absolutely no need to examine every small detail of the candlestick and try to fit it into the various different candlestick patterns on the textbook. There is no need to be over thinking when it comes to candlestick patterns.

In my book, when I see rough approximations to hammers or shooting stars, I accept them as it is and just add their signal into my overall aggregation of the decision for that particular counter.

There is also another candlestick pattern which I think is fairly important and that is called the doji. The doji looks like this.

+

A literal plus sign. This is a sign that the market is undecided and the bears and bulls have no power over each other. The usual stance when we see a doji would be to adopt a wait and see approach.

For me though, I like to think that every price chart is trying to tell a story, and a doji appearing at a crucial point may tell of something more significant than just simple indecision. Think about this, you have a stock that has been on the downward trend for some periods, and then a doji appears at a substantive price level. This tells us that there definitely is a pause in the downward momentum of the counter, but as to what the stock may do next would then depend on your knowledge of the strength of that price level.

A similar situation happening in a space that has no significant price levels would probably mean that the bears are just really taking a breather, and will continue the slaughter after having their rest.

This is how we start to piece and surmise things from the clues which the market provides us.

This is also the reason why I am of mind that you do not really have to know all the candlestick patterns. There is no need to create more potential confusion for yourself. To be honest, when I teach my folks, I just tell them to pay attention to the shooting star, the doji and the hammer.

That's it.

The shooting star and hammer represent the extremes and also the exhaustion of the prior trend, and hence it has quite a bit of power in foretelling a reversal in the direction of price, especially when the candle happens on a day, month or even a yearly candle. Remember, larger the time period, the stronger the signal.

The doji as I mentioned earlier, would be either indecision or a resting point, and that usually you have got to pair it with support and resistance bands in order to get better clarity on its true nature.

Having said all the above, I would also like to point out that candlestick patterns are meant to help and provide more clues for you to piece together a coherent, workable story regarding the stock in question. You are not going to pull the trigger based on the occurrence of a pattern.

Some course on price action do teach triggers via candlestick patterns, but for me, I don't practise it as such. Clues they are, and clues they shall remain. I prefer to have more information on hand before making any potential moves which involves my cash to be honest!

Periods

We have touched on this topic before in an earlier section but I would like to speak about this again with respect to its importance in the field of technical analysis. Periods are what we refer to as time periods. It can be as short as one minute, to an hour long, or as lengthy as a day or a month. This means that an entire candle is encapsulated in one month if we were looking at a monthly candlestick.

The longer the period, the more conviction and staying power it has for that candle, and hence the more valuable its accompanying signal will be. A trigger on a one minute candle would be much weaker when held against a trigger on a day candle. By this, we can simply think that it is much easier to trust the day candle versus the one minute candle. In a similar vein, it will be much easier to trust a month candle when it is held up against a day candle.

When we analyze charts, it is always good practice to zoom out straight to the largest time frame possible. For me, that usually means going straight to the month chart or even the yearly chart, where one candlestick represents one month or one year. This way of looking at things ensures that you have quite the macro view at the very start, which is always a good place to initiate your chart investigation. You want to use the clues on the chart to piece together a coherent story which will then help to structure an execution plan for the investment target.

Going in from the big time frames will also ensure that you will have the best opportunity to take a look at the history of the price movement. The up and downtrends of the stock should be evident, as well as potential sideways movement. Of course, our final object of interest will always be the movement area that is closest to the most recently presented candle on the chart itself. We want to see if it is an upward, downward or just a sideways kind of trend.

The beauty of a larger time frame chart is that these trends become much clearer as compared to when it is viewed on a lower timeframe. The old adage of trading with the trend holds some weight, and that is the reason why we would want to know what the stock is doing on the higher timeframe.

For many folks who are just starting out, or who may be already having some experience with charting, one of the most common issues would be the conflict between the lower and higher timeframes. What do I mean by this?

Imagine you have a chart which you are looking at it on the day period and it is telling you that it is a period of sideways movement. You want to double check on the higher time frame and see if there is coherence and you switch to the weekly chart. On the weekly chart you do see some evidence of sideways movement but you think that you need more confirmation because what you see does not seem to convince you thoroughly. You then move up to the monthly chart. When looking through the lens of a month chart, you see that the stock is in fact trending downwards. You then merge these two findings together and formulate a plan. A day sideways movement, coupled with a month downward trend would probably mean that you would have a higher probable win rate if you were to do short selling when the stock nears any resistance levels and to take quicker profit when it nears the support bands. The short selling is in line with the monthly downward trend, whilst the selling on the high and taking faster profit on the support level conforms to the day sideways trend.

This is also applicable when you are doing day trading. It is just that we zoom down to lower time frames. Usually we would look at the day chart to get a gist of how the overall trend is going to be like, then we would push further down into the hourly chart and then further down into the fifteen minute chart or the five minute chart for the actual triggering.

The principles are always the same, we want to move in accordance as much as possible with the higher time frame because that is what will give us more confidence. We can then utilize the lower time frames to pull our triggers for trade initiation.

Another thing I want to point out would be the trade-off. In situations where we wait to initiate or confirm trades on the higher time frame, that would also usually mean we would probably get in at a less advantageous price when compared to pulling the trigger on the signal from the lower time frame.

More confirmation would mean taking more time, which also means bearing the risk of having a lousier price to trigger your trade on. Going in on the lower time frames would mean quicker speed and in most cases better price in terms of trade execution, but it means bearing the risk that it could just be a fake signal and having the trade go south on you.

For me, I always would tend toward more confirmation, because I have had the experience of doing too many lower timeframe trades and I just did not really enjoy the taste of it.

I mean, automation is great these days, but for most retail players, we would still retain quite a bit of manual control on the trades. Triggering one trade based on the day chart sounds better to me versus fifteen trades based on the five minute chart. Of course, it goes back to your trading psyche as well. So if you are the adrenaline junkie kind, well, perhaps you might really get to enjoy punching in trades every five minutes, who knows!

What about getting in on the less favorable price you say? That is the reason why we call it the trade-off. More confirmation and you pay more in terms of the entry price. It is just like a concert where you have to pay more in order to be closer to the stage, where you can observe the action much closer and better.

Personally, there is part of my trading persona where I know that I am pretty cool if I don't get the trade, because I can simply wait for the next better one. I know for certain there will always be a next one coming, in part because of my trust in my system, and also because I have been seeing it work for that many years. With this little facet of my trading psychology, I then devise a workaround with regards to the less favorable price upon higher timeframe confirmation.

When I first see the trigger on the higher timeframe, I will not execute a market order. This means I do not just jump in at the price which is the current market price. I will take a look at the nearest, logical support or resistance level and then park a limit order which will usually get me a better price as compared to the market price.

This means I do not get the luxury of having exposure in the trade call by doing the market order, but instead I choose to trade that luxury for a better price entry and it is somewhat of a side bet that I judge the price would retrace back to my limit orders.

This also means that on some occasions, I will have to totally forgo the trade altogether because the price just does not retrace back to any of my limit orders. In the case of a bullish trade, the stock price just zooms straight up with nary a look backwards, and I can just wave forlornly goodbye in the distance. I mean I used to, not anymore these days.

This method is pretty much a double or nothing mentality, which I personally use to circumvent the issue of having to pay too much in order to initiate a trade or investment.

It can also be pretty trying at times, because you could have set your limit buy orders for example, and the stock price moves up, and it could be days or weeks even, before it finally decides to come back down and touch your limits. During that interim period, you might be emotionally roller-coastered, so it might be a good idea to really get a grip on your trading psychology and emotions first before deciding if this method is one which you might be tempted to try.

Of course, when it works, you get the satisfaction of having the right trade, with the added conviction of the higher timeframe signal, as well as a pretty good price to boot. This would also mean more profit margins for you due to the larger differential between the entry and target profit price.

When it doesn't work, I just dust it off and carry on to the next trade. You cannot win all of them, and the danger in trying to do so far outstrips any potential rewards it may offer.

So for this topic of timeframe, it is most important that I impress upon you the value of the higher timeframe chart. You can start by zooming straight to the higher timeframe whenever you are analyzing any stock chart, as this will put your mind in a macro frame so you will be seeing the bigger picture.

During my earlier trainings, I used to flip through countless higher timeframe charts of different companies, and observe how companies in the same industries might have similar chart movements, while others may have their differences as well. For those with the same movements, you would also notice the movement direction may be the same for the similar time period, but the degree of movement would have their nuanced differences.

Another interesting facet would be spotting a company in the same industry that has different chart movement from all its major competitors, and that would be a clue worthy of further investigation. Some of the hidden gems might be just hiding in plain sight for all we know, and it just needs a little more probing to let it see the light.

There is no running away from effort and work when it comes to all forms of stock and investment analysis. I guess that is the ultimate message which I would like to send across to you or anyone reading this. Stock chart reading is a skill, just like riding a bicycle or fishing.

It can be learnt and picked up, further ruminated upon and polished into an art form.

This is the reason why some folks may just take a glance at a price chart and know in an instant if there is any opportunity or not. They have majored this form of analysis into a skill that is close to an art form, and at times, they may find it hard to explain their decisions to others. This was what happened to me when I was first apprenticing under one of my mentors. He was someone so ingrained in the market that it seemed he was operating on feeling and intuition. His most common phrase to me during my tutelage was "it's very simple, as plain as day".

Of course, I struggled with that every single time he uttered those words. I simply could not see what he was seeing and it was really some time and effort later which then let me discover my stock charting eyes.

So, take heart if it looks all mumbo jumbo to you at the present, because there really is a light at the end of the tunnel, and it is honestly a question of you finishing that walk down the tunnel and emerging well into the sunshine. It can be done. Just stick to the principles and stay hungry to better yourself. You will be fine.

Alright, that was a slight pep talk, so back to the other aspects of technical analysis which I find important.

Wave Theory

Some of you may have heard of the intriguing theory called Elliot Wave theory. The long and short of it is these waves are supposed to be extremely predictive in nature, and that means if you manage to master reading Elliot waves, you are thus able to trade and invest with ease.

Generally, in an uptrend, you should have five waves, and then when it comes to a retracement, there should be three waves. This makes for a total of eight waves for an up movement, with its accompanying draw down. The same goes for a downtrend. The downward portion will have five waves while its retracement will also be spotted as having three waves.

Sounds good right?

One big nefarious issue here is this. There seems to be no logical base for getting started with your wave one. That means any place can be deemed as the start of wave one, and you can imagine the messy disputes when various Elliot wave technicians meet each other.

The other big issue with wave theory is that it is very much a fractal concept. This means, in a major up wave one, you will also have within that single one wave, a whole set of five waves up and three waves down.

And this can literally keep on going down to the smaller time periods.

As one who has tried his hand in pure Elliot wave counting, I can assure you that I have not really mastered it. There simply seems to be so many different starting points and I have absolutely no idea as to which wave should belong to which.

Maybe others have had better results with it, but so far I have not really seen anyone doing that well with just pure Elliot wave counting.

Why are we then talking about waves, if there seem to be so many diverse issues surrounding its proper usage? The key reason is this, we need a basic understanding of waves in order to help us with the chart reading.

You can ignore the portions about wave counting and all its associated burdens, but the crux that you have to catch would be the actual visual recognition of a wave when presented to you on the candlestick chart. The whole purpose of getting to know Elliot wave is simply to let us get more acquainted with the visual aspects of seeing and recognizing the up and down waves as shown via the price movements.

On one hand, I see some folks heaving a sigh of relief that they do not have to step into that confusing mire that is actual Elliot wave counting, while on the other hand, I also see some people questioning if this is it? The whole purpose of knowing wave theory is just so that you get a better visual yardstick with which you use for charting.

The simple answer is yes. It really is for that purpose. To be frank, some people actually try to automate this wave charting process, but I find that the analysis produced to be of a distinct inferior vintage as compared to the manual, visual process.

One of the things which actually help with wave recognition is the definition of an up and down trend.

For an uptrend, you should be seeing higher price points than its previous high, while seeing higher lows as compared to its previous lows. The crux of the uptrend is always its higher lows. An uptrend which is obvious will have higher highs to complement those higher lows, but it can also have stagnant highs as well. This means we see a kind of flat plateau of price highs, with its accompanying higher price lows. This also qualifies as an uptrend too.

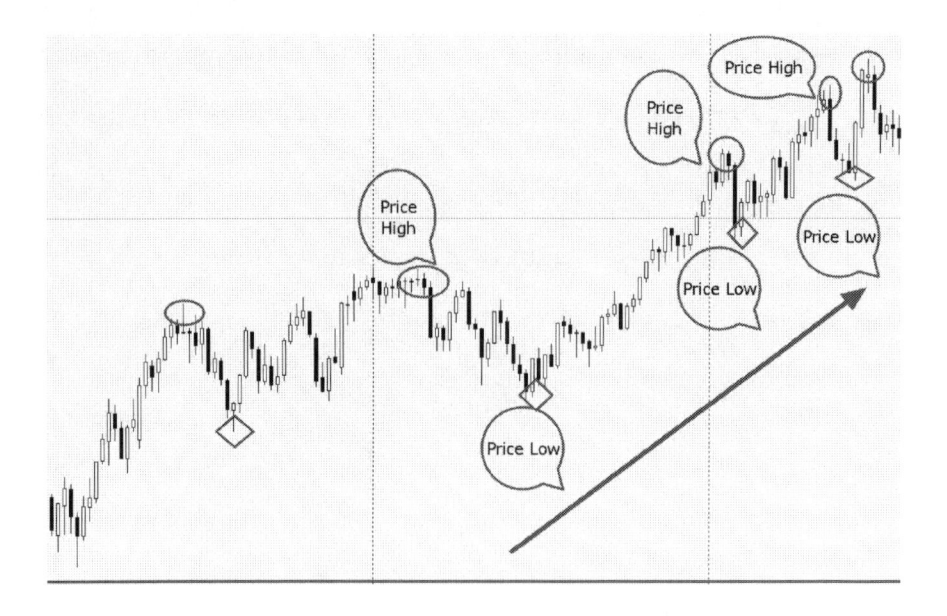

For the downtrend, the reverse will be true. Lower price highs will be the key here as well, while lower price lows will be present in a straight forward downtrend. It is essentially the uptrend in reverse. In order to verify that a downtrend is indeed happening on a stock or counter, we want to spot its lower highs. In the event that the price lows are all staying flat without putting up a show of reaching for lower lows, it still qualifies as a downtrend as long as the lower highs are in place. What happens if we see a situation where there are lower highs, and yet the stock also displays higher lows? This then becomes a strike out from the downtrend definition, and you would not be advised to classify the price movement as that of a downward trend any longer.

The same situation goes for the uptrend. Should you observe higher lows, while there is also a formation of lower highs ongoing, then the classification of upward trend should no longer be labelled onto that particular stock.

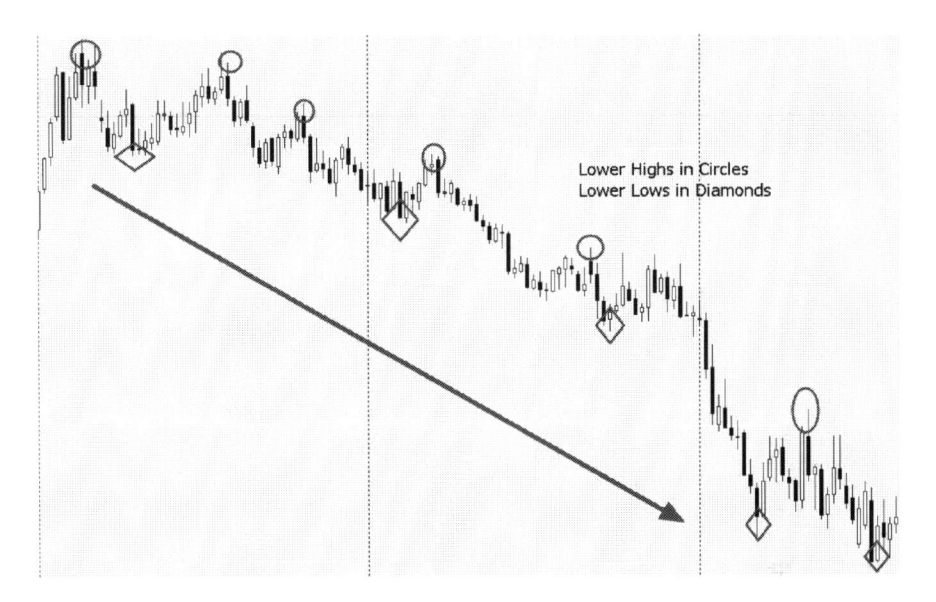

Lower Highs in Circles
Lower Lows in Diamonds

When you have the concepts of up and downtrend firmly in place, you would be in a much better place to recognize the price movements when they form in relation to the candlesticks.

There might be an inclination to overanalyze initially, especially when it comes to folks who are beginners. It is wholly normal to do that, but it is definitely not encouraged. I would have to say the overzealous analysis would somehow pave the way for faster and more accurate recognition of the waves within the price movements.

For me, I literally looked at charts for hours on end, and coupled that with actual live trading as well so that each trade becomes a teacher on its own. When folks practise stock market investing and charting in this manner, the experiential process is much stronger and you actually might learn faster.

I will come right out and say as I always do, that there is no immediate shortcut to success with regards to this. I have seen some folks pick it up very quickly, like in a few short months they are able to grasp the finer details and concepts and more importantly utilize it firmly for their own charting purposes. There are others who are a tad slower, and their learning process may take upwards of a year or so.

Regardless of which it may be for yourself, it would be wise to note that everyone's learning process will be different, and slow or fast does not necessarily mean for the better. I can be numbered amongst those that needed a year or so in order to truly see the price movements for what they were, and I would say it did me no great harm putting in those extra hours because it served to deepen my knowledge on the workings of the stock market.

When we examine price waves, and delve further into the trends, we will invariably encounter chart patterns along the way. I shall not be touching too much into this topic at this juncture, because I believe them to be more suitable for a book that is dedicated more toward the technical analysis side of things. We can however, touch a little before we move on to the next major topic.

Remember the example I gave about the up and downtrends? Recall also the part where I mentioned for the case of an uptrend, and you start seeing higher lows as well as lower highs? That is in fact an example of a chart pattern called the symmetric triangle.

For the case when you have higher lows but encounter a plateau of similar highs, this will also be a chart pattern called the ascending triangle.

For the reverse situation where you see lower highs and same lows, this will be a chart pattern called descending triangle.

Though all are triangles, you do not treat them the same way. The central theme to triangles is that traditional investing and trading lore would say that these patterns indicate a compression of impetus and momentum, hence triangles always represent price break outs. We should expect to see strong movements in price when these patterns eventually bear fruit.

The way to trade them, however, is not the same.

For ascending and descending triangles, because we can still label them as being up or downtrends, the expectation would be for prices to continue on in their previous direction. An ascending triangle would see price break up, while a descending triangle would see price break down.

For the symmetric triangle, this is a bit trickier because the price can move either way. It can turn out to be what the folks call a continuation pattern, in which the price continues on its previous trajectory, or it may evolve to become a reversal pattern. In this case, the price will execute a sharp reverse of its previous heading. Up becomes down and down become up.

The traditional way of trading these triangles mostly involves trading on the breakout. This means you wait for the price candle to close above the line that you draw when you trace the shape of the triangle using its corresponding candlesticks. Some will advocate waiting for three candlesticks after the initial break. This all depends on the time frame which you are looking at to be honest. If you are already on the day candlestick, I would reckon that one single candle close would be more than sufficient to guard yourself against an instance of a fake price breakout. For folks on the lower time frame, then perhaps waiting for one or three more candlesticks would be somewhat prudent.

Again, there is the trade-off present here again. The more confirmation you want, the higher probability you have got to pay a higher entry price. In the days when I was trading breakouts without the use of price levels, I circumvented this issue by parking the limit orders again.

Yes, those limit orders again.

I have got to say they are pretty useful, and the benefits of using them more than outweigh the cost of missing out the trade in my opinion.

These days, I do not just jump into a trade whenever I see triangles. It is always good to pair chart patterns with the corresponding support and resistance levels in order to derive a better probability winning trade.

This is also what I would term as the danger contained within the usage of chart patterns for execution purposes. Once you start looking for patterns, you can literally see them anywhere, on any time frame. Try it! You won't be disappointed and can almost always spot any chart pattern.

This will present an ever present temptation to trade each and every chart pattern, and that is not what I would recommend. I did that before, and it was both exhausting as well as not rewarding. Chart patterns have a lot more significance when they are forming or formed on significant price levels, and it would be good to use chart patterns as yet another clue for the analysis of a potential trade or investment idea.

These days, I don't execute based on chart patterns alone. They serve me more as confirmatory as well as early warning signals for any stocks that I might be monitoring. Having a chart pattern form on any of your filtered stocks should be good news, either to warn against entry for now, or to support the decision to take exposure.

To sum up this segment, looking at how the price move and formulating an understanding of it within the structure of waves, up and downtrend movements would be crucial to develop further understanding for stock market analysis. With this analysis, it would then create a much better informed environment in order to make buy and sell calls.

Stock market investment does not always remain difficult. It is a subject that rewards people who constantly put in effort to understand and learn. In time, analysis becomes much quicker and more accurate, while the win ratio for your trade and investment calls will see an uptick. Also, when you trade better, your understanding of your personal trading psychology will also naturally blossom. This will stand you in good stead in daily life as well, because you will possess an awareness of your personal mental and emotional triggers, which may allow you to steer clear of potential future pitfalls.

Fibonacci

Here it is necessary for us to take a little history lesson. Truth be told, it is not an absolute must, but it would be good to know the related history so that we have a bit more grounding on this matter.

Fibonacci is the result of shortening filius Bonacci, which actually means the son of Bonaccio. This son would actually be Leonardo of Pisa, or more accurately, Leonardo Pisano Bigollo. He was an extraordinarily talented mathematician of his time. Born in Pisa in the year 1175, he had to his name quite a few mathematical breakthroughs, among which was the singular successful push for the Hindu-Arabic numeral system to be used in place of the Roman system. If not for him, we might be still dealing with those cumbersome Vs and Xs!

His other more important contribution to us is of course the development of the Fibonacci series or sequence. For the more academically inclined, the number sequence goes like this.

0, 1, 1, 2, 3, 5, 8, 13, 21, 34, 55, 89, 144, 233, 377, 610…… and so on.

The key here in finding the next number is adding up the previous two preceding numbers. So 0 plus 1 would give 1, while 1 plus 1 would give 2, 2 plus 1 would give 3 and so on.

The above were the prelude to the more important stuff, which namely was the golden ratio in the form of 1.618 or 0.618. So what happened was as the Fibonacci sequence continued on to ever larger numbers, one realizes that if we were to take 610 and divide it by 377, we would get the ratio 1.618. You can try this with the larger numbers in the sequence. In fact, the ratio starts to exert itself when you get to divisions from the number 21 onwards.

What's so special about the golden ratio? Many folk have realized that the ratio can be found on our own anatomies, the length of our arms in ratio to our entire body length would be of the 0.618 proportion. Flipping it over, it would mean that our body's length in relation to our arms would be 1.618. Not stopping at that, the 1.618 phenomena can be found in the nautilus shell, the sunflower as well as a whole host of nature's creations. It is also said that attractive people often have the golden ratio in built onto their facial features. Something about the length of the cheek bones to the entire length of the face or something along those lines. Whatever it is, it has become a recognized fact that the golden ratio is indeed present in many of nature's creations and hence the next logical step is to elude it as being part of the cycle of life.

When this is so, we would then come to utilize the numbers 0.618 and 1.618 and its variants onto the stock market. The stock market is indeed a reflection or a microcosm of life, and that is why earlier stock market practitioners have sought to use the golden ratio as a way to peer forward with regards to the price movements.

For me, I am happy with reading about history and all, because firstly I am kind of a history buff, and secondly it just fascinates me to look at how certain stock market methodologies are actually derived. Yet, the most important facet of the impact Fibonacci numbers, or more accurately the golden ratio has on the stock market would be the fact that they actually work.

At least in my opinion.

In the stock market, we are primarily concerned with the ratios of 0.618 and 1.618. These would be known as the Fibonacci extensions if you were to look them up on any charting software. There are other Fibonacci ratios like 0.382 and 0.236 which may commonly appear as what we call Fibonacci retracement numbers. We do not really concern ourselves with those. Our primary targets would be 0.618 as well as the 1.618 projections.

Why so?

The simple answer is to avoid over analysis as well as the over cluttering of your chart with too many different lines. Any chart that has too many different lines, without allowing the practitioner to get a clear picture of what is happening with the stock is actually not a good chart. I was guilty of that early on, when I would have Fibonacci retracements, chart pattern lines and suspected round number price levels all drawn onto the chart.

This creates a very messy situation, and also begs the question of which price level would be deemed the more important ones. Would that be the extension lines arising from the chart pattern? Or would it be the Fibonacci retracement ratios? That is the reason why I choose to stick to 0.618 and 1.618 because I have come to realize these are the more potent and accurate numbers.

The next big issue faced with using Fibonacci would be the fact that many folks would often ask, where would they start and end the retracement? This is a big conundrum that actually has nothing to do with the efficacy of Fibonacci retracements or extensions.

The trick to this seemingly big issue would be to locate the turning points that are presented on the price chart. Turning points are points where the price turns from up to down, or vice versa. This usually means if a stock has been trending down, and then makes a U-turn to reverse upward and start climbing up, that particular area where the U-turn has been made would be a proper turning point. This portion would tie in with our advice on using the bigger time frames. When you are on the bigger time frames like the week or the month chart, the tendency to be able to spot price turning points would be higher.

Again, this is something which will get better with practice, and it will be a good idea to start off the practising using the higher time frame charts. Once you get the hang of spotting the turning points, then it would be good to pop down to the lower time frame charts in order to have a closer glimpse on the more recent price action.

When turning points are confirmed, the placement of the start and end of the Fibonacci retracements would be an easy task. Most major charting software, both online and offline would definitely have this tool within their range of tools. You will then be able to see the reaction of the stock price on certain Fibonacci levels like the 0.618 and 0.386. If the price has not reached those levels, they will be good places to observe how the price moves and also to plan ahead on potential trades.

In my intermediate career, when I still use the Fibonacci retracements, what I would do would be this. I'd locate the turning points, usually at least on the weekly chart first, then draw in the retracements, paying much attention to the 0.618. I would then zoom down into the day chart when the action starts to head toward the weekly 0.618 line. On the day chart, I would be checking out the nearest turning points with which to draw out my retracements. So it would be a situation where I would have both a weekly retracement level, and also a daily chart retracement level. If it were an up trending stock, I would usually look to initiate a purchase on the day chart 0.618 level.

One of the things which I absolutely love, and when that happens, I would take the trade more often than not, would be when there is a confluence of Fibonacci lines. This means that the weekly Fibonacci lines coincide with the daily Fibonacci lines. On occasions when those corresponding lines happen to be both the 0.618, it is pretty much a good bet that there would definitely be a reaction there when the stock price hits the area.

The crux of using Fibonacci to trade and invest lies in the waiting for reaction when the stock price reaches the Fibonacci levels. On "weaker" Fibonacci levels, where you might be expecting a bounce, the price may just fall through and go on downwards. That is also part of the reason why I choose to pay most of my attention to 0.618 and 1.618 these days.

Another thing to note here would be, the above which I just described was what transpired during my intermediate years of investing journey. It is worth a note that I don't really use that methodology any more.

These days, I actually rely more on Fibonacci extensions that are combined with price turning points, but that is going to be another story for another book. I reckon that will be a tome which would go into details on my trading and investing process, the nuts and bolts so to speak, so the only thing I can say here is, please be on the lookout for it.

At this point in time, it might be a little overwhelming for the true beginner, or it could be a little deflating for the journeyman. I would like to take this opportunity to state that this is how I would feel too after reading books on trading and investing. There seems to be no quick method to riches, and yet there looks to be much to do if one were to be looking for consistent profits in the stock market.

A lot of the success that you experience with investing in the stock market starts with the amount of time you actually invest in yourself. The time to go through financial reports, the time to look at the price charts and the time to honestly assess your own trading psyche.

I cannot stress again that there simply is no quick fix, or perhaps it might be out there somewhere, but I just cannot find it yet. Just like the pot of gold at the end of the rainbow. That pot of gold, however, will have a higher probability of being there at the end of the learning journey to investing in the stock market where you put in the hours and never give up.

CHAPTER 6

Rule Number Six (Constant Profits)

This portion will be detailing the way to go in order to get ahead in terms of profiting from the stock market. Many a time, we always hear things like:

- Many investors fail in making money from the stock market, even more so for retail players
- You might win for a little, but the house always wins in the end
- It is better off placing your trust in mutual funds and highly paid professionals

In most marketing material for expensive stock trading and investment courses, this would be the time where the material would state categorically that they have the special answer that would allow you to be the special one or ten percent that would be able to consistently beat the market, reap in the passive profits, all on the easy investment of one hour a day.

Sounds good right?

The fact of the matter is many retail players do lose money, but a lot do make money as well, and the only people who will ever really know for sure would be the folks in the tax department. Like I have mentioned, the road to earning and profiting from the stock market lies primarily with yourself.

You have to put in the time and effort in order to learn and understand how the market works in order to have a fighting chance to beat it on a consistent basis. Here, we will examine some pointers that will be helpful in launching you toward profitability.

Do Not Follow The Herd

This principle is oft a simple but overlooked one when dealing with matters of investing in the stock market. It is often easy to fall prey to the general tide of emotions when it comes to precious stock tips and so called insider news. You want to get into the thick of it and would definitely fear missing out on what you perceive as golden opportunities to make quick and effortless profits.

Banish those thoughts.

In not following the herd, we are actually looking at this from two subtly different angles. In one, we do not allow ourselves to be pulled and swayed by the easy seduction of stock tips by so called experts. In the other, we do not base our own investing decisions purely on what the general crowd is currently doing. At its core, we will always rely on our own judgement, formulated from the rigorous fundamental and technical forms of analysis, in order to filter and make the necessary sale and purchase decisions.

This is not to say that we are not open to ideas which may come from others. That is definitely not so. It is imperative to keep an open mind, the better which to learn with. My take on this would be to look upon potential ideas gleaned from others as just that – potential ideas. They still need to be subject to the filtration and analytical process which form the core of the investing career. In periods of extreme emotion, the temptation to be swept up by the raw energy of greed or fear would be great, but please do your best to stave it off. You will find yourself better off for it.

For me, I have always found it easier to ignore stock calls during periods of a bull run, when virtually every second person you meet on the streets would be eager to share about investing, and to offer their bit of well-meaning sage advice. I suppose there lies in me an inner skeptic, waiting to pounce at the slightest opportunity. Beyond that personal slant, would be the grounding that I have in the system of analysis which I have come to rely on to make all of my investing decisions.

I know that even if this recommended stock call was to do superbly well, and for some reason or another, my analysis did not lead me to take any action, there would be other more definite opportunities awaiting me. That reduces the fear of missing out to virtually zero.

For the situations when the bear market arises, it is usually fear that is more dominant in such cases. Many a time, people would be handing out advice to stay out of the stock market, or to get out of a particular stock before it becomes all too late. The fear I find it harder to handle than the greed, which is normal. That is also part of the reason why bear markets are often swifter in their build up as compared to their bull counterparts. People are more easily motivated by fear than by greed.

The way to combat this is also to stay focused and steadfast on your method of analysis. For me, I know that any decision I make will be a result of fundamental and technical analysis, and that gives me conviction to see out the decision. This leads in to the next point on your system.

Trust Your System

When you trust your system, you will be able to be at ease whether it is a bear or bull market. This is because you have the trust and knowledge that your system will be generating its consistent share of opportunities for you to move toward profitability.

A thing to note here though, is that you do not just cobble any old set of technical indicators and then call that your system. I used to do that in the early stages, and it was a frequent sight where I bailed from my investing decisions, often at critical junctures which would have seen me making profits instead of the frequent losses.

When I speak of the system, it is something like what I have created for myself. For me, I utilize a two-step process which lets the fundamental analysis do the stock filtration, then the technical analysis to spot optimal entry and exit points. Some folks deal build their systems entirely based on technical analysis, while others just stick to the fundamentals. There is no right or wrong answer. I suppose the most realistic way to look at this would be whichever system that lets you generate consistent profits over a reasonable amount of time would be considered the right system for you.

For me, I find that marrying the two big schools of analysis works out pretty well, and it gives me a sense of security knowing that most of the angles should be covered. You have to decide what would work for you when you are constructing your preferred system.

The fundamental side of things have their positives, as do technical analysis of stocks. They also have their share of problems too. No one system can ever claim blatant superiority over the other, which is probably the reason why the one I utilize now draws elements from both instead.

In your creation of your own preferred system, you may find that you have the same thoughts and experiences as myself, and hence create an amalgamation of the fundamental and technical. In other cases, you could be much tilted toward the technical side of things, and your system could resemble something of a mathematical model. Whichever the case may be, the step following the assembly of your system, would be the rigorous testing of it.

This is where you build your trust.

Back testing is often the most common way which people employ to check the efficacy and profitability of a system. This method is easy to deploy with purely technical systems, because these days, the test results can be gotten within a matter of minutes. For the fundamentalist, it is also possible to back test, but it will have to be more manual in nature. They would have to check the stock price movement in relation to the quarterly or annual reports. Back testing is good for creating a basis for a system, but another form of testing will be needed to stress proof it.

Forward testing, or testing in real time, would be the usage of the system in either mock or live trading. This kind of testing would capture the emotions of the unknown as well as the associated feelings when the call is subsequently proven correct or wrong. I did forward testing for my system for almost close to a year before increasing the stakes on each investing decision.

The downside to forward testing is that it literally takes time. There is no shortcut to it. The great thing about this is that you will build a solid belief in your system if you see it work consistently. Even if the system ultimately does not work, you would have gain precious knowledge in tinkering with it and coming away with more ideas on how to make it work for you.

At this point, I would think that you can probably get away with doing forward testing for about six months. When it comes to this matter, I would say that the longer the period, the better it would be. This has, of course, got to be balanced with the problem of what happens if the system just does not work. This then comes back to the important question of how you formulate your system.

Take for example a person who decides that he would like to invest based on momentum. He crafts a simple system where he would go long or purchase a stock if its price breaks the 52 week high price watermark. For him, because this is quite a simple system, he will be able to do back testing on this methodology to check on its usefulness. If he is satisfied with the back test results, he can then move it on to the forward testing phase, where he is able to examine the results first hand. He will have to start thinking of the practical aspects of this methodology, because he will have some experience wielding it during the live trading period. He might ponder on the issue of deciding which stock to invest in, since there could be many stocks which break their 52 week high watermark in the same instant. He will also be looking at the overall profitability of this methodology, and making notes on whether it is worthwhile to pursue this track.

In general, the system does not have to be very complicated. It just has to make sense to you and of course, ultimately be profitable when it is used in the markets.

Market Timing

If you want to achieve supernormal returns on the stock market, then I don't care what other people say, market timing will be a skill that you have to master.

There will always be a time to buy stocks, and a time to sell them. A profitable venture into the stock market would need someone to take advantage of those two optimal timings, and have the heart to see it through.

Can you hope to achieve returns if you just want to get into a stock and hold it for posterity? The answer is yes. You can indeed, but the chances of getting supernormal returns would be tougher. There are many stories and investing lore that abound with people who invested $5,000 and gotten a million dollars back after 30 years. What these stories do not mention would be that these investments were in companies that were the next big wave. It is something like getting into Apple or any of the tech giants in early 2000.

It is not an everyday affair that opportunities like these abound, and once missed, it could very well be a wait that lasts a generation. It is to circumvent this issue that I put forth the notion of market timing. When you are able to capture the peaks and troughs of the market, you do not need to always hit the jackpot when it comes to company selection.

Also, it is also good to put aside the idea that you will be purchasing at the very bottom and selling at the absolute top. Not many people can do that. In fact, at this point of writing, I have not seen any one who can lay claim to doing it consistently and conscientiously. More often than not, we would be seeing hitting the seventy fifth percentile mark as a good achievement. Selling the stock when it is a quarter move away from the very top, and buying the stock when it is a quarter move away from the very bottom, to me, are laudable accomplishments that would probably need some years of practice.

The other reason why market timing is somewhat crucial to achieving the supernormal returns that most would crave for in the stock market, is the fact that we have to account for the churning effect.

If a stock were to experience a 100 point rise in the space of three years, that would be deemed in most quarters as quite a good investment. If I were to propose getting five different instances of 20 point rise within a space of a year, would that be plausible? First off, a 20 point rise would have a higher probability of occurrence as compared to a 100 point rise. Secondly, I would just have to find five different instances where there is a higher probability of seeing a 20 point move. Also, finding five 20 point moves in a year would be probably easier than finding one 100 point move in one or two years. The point I am making is that with market timing, you are probably going to chalk up a higher aggregate of gains across a larger number of investments as compared to having all your gains centered on one or two companies.

Market timing would metaphorically allow you to earn a dollar from every person on the planet as compared to earning ten dollars from everyone in your country. When you think about it, would it be easier to get someone to give you a dollar as opposed to getting someone to part with ten dollars? The same thing goes for a stock. It would be a trifle more difficult to bag a tenbagger, as some of the Wall Street folks would put it, as compared to getting yourself constant onebaggers. For clarification purposes, one bag is equivalent to one fold increment of the stock price. This is one of the main reasons why I would deem market timing as one of the skills which you probably have to pick up as you progress along in your stock investing career.

Again, as with many things in life and also in the markets, nothing is absolutely carved in stone or rock. There are usually at least two sides to everything, and sometimes maybe more than two. For this matter of market timing, despite my continued exhortations for one to pick this useful skill up, I do acknowledge that for some, it might be actually wasteful for them to learn this skill.

For the people who are already guardians or husbanders of great amounts of resource and capital, I would then feel that the skill of market timing might not be as crucial to them as it would be to the normal retail investor. For these folks endowed with extraordinarily large amounts of resources, they can really adopt a purchase and hold strategy which may last for generations. This is because their immediate needs are already well met with whatever monies they have on hand, and the huge surplus will be directed toward investments which literally can be afforded lifetimes to bear fruit.

Not everyone is a scion of such family wealth or possesses the opportunity to acquire a vast amount of money within a really short time. Quite a large number of us still work to get the cash rolling in, and it is quite on the top of most minds as to how best to generate more returns for the surplus savings.

At the end of the day, using market timing correctly and with the proper application, would then allow one to hasten the rate of compounding for one's capital.

Conclusion

And so we reach this juncture, where it is customarily thought that most readers of this genre would be chomping at the bit, to be let loose on the stock market. I advise caution in this case, and if you have been following all the prior chapters closely, you would also have arrived at the same conclusions as myself.

The market is precisely that – a market. There is no emotion, no attachment to it. There is nothing romantic about it, nor is it particularly exciting. The great issue for most is that many tend to mix the stock market up with money, or more precisely, money which they hope to own.

Please step away from that pedestal, and turn your thoughts away from that.

The more you are able to stay dispassionate and relatively cool with regards to the workings and machinations of the stock market or any market of assets, the better it would be for your overall investing endeavour.

To me, the correct application of this book for the seasoned journeyman or for the beginner would be always to go back to the basics. Get a good grasp of the kind of market that you are dealing with. For example, if you should decide that you would like to confine your hunt to just the S&P 500 index stocks, then study those stocks and come to understand the index's movement like you would your own body. This of course, does not happen overnight, and it would require daily conscientious effort in order to work towards it.

With the clarity of targets, the next step would be to formulate your hunting strategy or hunting system. This is where loads of people would be gunning for the easy way out, seduced by this or that readymade system sold by glib salespeople who promise the rolling in of riches with the investment of just an hour a day.

Nothing worthwhile is ever for free. Just think of the duck floating serenely on the surface of the lake, when it is actually paddling constantly to keep afloat beneath the waters. So too should this be a harbinger for how the construction of your personal system be like.

You may run into dead ends, and may even start tearing your hair out from their roots in frustration. That is normal. What matters most at this point would be the tenacious continuation of the search to create your own workable system. I can only say to you – Do Not Give Up.

You will be able to find that system eventually, and when you trust it and start seeing the consistent profits from it, that would make all the prior frustrations very worth their while.

It is my sincerest wish that you would be able to generate consistent returns from the stock market, and who knows, perhaps one day you would be able to quit your day job and enjoy life solely off the profits from the stock market.

Never give up.

At this stage

I would like to seek some help from you

Please just leave a review for this book on one or more Useful things

which you picked up.

Thank You Very Much!

Manufactured by Amazon.ca
Bolton, ON